ECONOMIC ISSUES, PROBLEMS AND PERSPECTIVES

FEDERAL DEBT, INTEREST COSTS AND THE DEBT LIMIT

ECONOMIC ISSUES, PROBLEMS AND PERSPECTIVES

Additional books in this series can be found on Nova's website under the Series tab.

Additional E-books in this series can be found on Nova's website under the E-books tab.

ECONOMIC ISSUES, PROBLEMS AND PERSPECTIVES

FEDERAL DEBT, INTEREST COSTS AND THE DEBT LIMIT

ANTHONY V. MARTINEZ
AND
KAREN M. SCHULZ
EDITORS

Nova Science Publishers, Inc.
New York

For permission to use material from this book please contact us:
Telephone 631-231-7269; Fax 631-231-8175
Web Site: http://www.novapublishers.com

Additional color graphics may be available in the e-book version of this book.

Library of Congress Cataloging-in-Publication Data

Federal debt, interest costs, and the debt limit / editors, Anthony V. Martinez and Karen M. Schulz.
p. cm.
Includes index.
ISBN 978-1-61324-288-9 (softcover)
1. Debts, Public--United States. 2. Interest rates--United States. I. Martinez, Anthony V. II. Schulz, Karen M. III. Title.

HJ8119.F3954 2011
336.3'4350973--dc22

2011010127

Published by Nova Science Publishers, Inc. † New York

CONTENTS

PREFACE

The past few years have seen a sharp rise in the debt of the federal government. The surge in debt stems partially from lower tax revenues and higher federal spending related to the recent severe recession and turmoil in financial markets. However, the growing debt also reflects an imbalance between spending and revenues that predated those economic developments. This book examines federal debt issues and interest costs, as well as a history of the debt limit.

Chapter 1- The past few years have seen a sharp rise in the debt of the federal government. At the end of fiscal year 2008, debt held by the public amounted to $5.8 trillion—equal to 40 percent of the nation's annual economic output (gross domestic product, or GDP), a little above the 40-year average of 35 percent.[1] Since then, debt held by the public has shot upward, surpassing $9 trillion by the end of fiscal year 2010—equal to 62 percent of GDP, the highest percentage since shortly after World War II. The surge in debt stems partly from lower tax revenues and higher federal spending related to the recent severe recession and turmoil in financial markets. However, the growing debt also reflects an imbalance between spending and revenues that predated those economic developments.

Chapter 2- Total debt of the federal government can increase in two ways. First, debt increases when the government sells debt to the public to finance budget deficits and acquire the financial resources needed to meet its obligations. This increases *debt held by the public*. Second, debt increases when the federal government issues debt to certain government accounts, such as the Social Security, Medicare, and Transportation trust funds, in exchange for their reported surpluses. This increases *debt held by government accounts*. The sum of *debt held by the public* and *debt held by government accounts* is the total federal debt. Surpluses reduce debt held by the public, while deficits raise it. Total federal debt outstanding was $14,025 billion on December 31, 2010. The U.S. Treasury projects the federal debt will reach its statutory limit in spring 2011, although tax policy, spending changes, and economic trends, will affect that timing. Without a debt limit increase, funding federal operations after the middle of 2011 may be complicated.

In: Federal Debt, Interest Costs... ISBN: 978-1-61324-288-9
Editors: A. V. Martinez, K. M. Schulz

Chapter 1

FEDERAL DEBT AND INTEREST COSTS*

Congress of The United States; Congressional Budget Office

INTRODUCTION

Recently, the federal government has been recording the largest budget deficits, as a share of gross domestic product (GDP), since the end of World War II. As a result of those deficits, the amount of federal debt held by the public has soared—surpassing $9 trillion at the end of fiscal year 2010 and equal to 62 percent of GDP. The interest the government pays on that debt is currently low by historical standards as a percentage of GDP but is expected to grow rapidly over the next several years as interest rates rise. In response to a request from the Chairman and Ranking Member of the Senate Budget Committee, this study provides background material on federal debt and interest costs.

Jared Brewster and Amber Marcellino of the Congressional Budget Office's (CBO's) Budget Analysis Division wrote the study under the supervision of Theresa Gullo and Jeffrey Holland. Jared Brewster wrote the Summary and Chapters 1 and 2; Amber Marcellino and Jared Brewster wrote

* This is an edited, reformatted and augmented version of a Congress of The United States; Congressional Budget Office's publication, dated December 2010.

Chapter 3. Jonathan Huntley and Avi Lerner of CBO also contributed to the study. Staff of the Office of Management and Budget provided valuable assistance. (The assistance of external participants implies no responsibility for the final product, which rests solely with the authors and CBO.)

Sherry Snyder edited the manuscript, Kate Kelly proofread it, Jeanine Rees prepared the study for publication, and Maureen Costantino designed the cover. Monte Ruffin oversaw the printing of the study, Linda Schimmel handled the print distribution, and Simone Thomas prepared the electronic version for CBO's Web site (www.cbo.gov).

Douglas W. Elmendorf Director
December 2010

SUMMARY

The past few years have seen a sharp rise in the debt of the federal government. At the end of fiscal year 2008, debt held by the public amounted to $5.8 trillion—equal to 40 percent of the nation's annual economic output (gross domestic product, or GDP), a little above the 40-year average of 35 percent.[1] Since then, debt held by the public has shot upward, surpassing $9 trillion by the end of fiscal year 2010—equal to 62 percent of GDP, the highest percentage since shortly after World War II (see Summary Figure 1). The surge in debt stems partly from lower tax revenues and higher federal spending related to the recent severe recession and turmoil in financial markets. However, the growing debt also reflects an imbalance between spending and revenues that predated those economic developments.

At the same time, a sharp drop in interest rates has held down the amount of interest that the government pays on that debt. In 2010, net interest outlays totaled $197 billion, or 1.4 percent of GDP—a smaller share of GDP than they accounted for during most of the past decade.

The Congressional Budget Office (CBO) projects that, under current law, debt held by the public will exceed $16 trillion by 2020, reaching nearly 70 percent of GDP. CBO also projects that interest rates will go up. The combination of rising debt and rising interest rates is projected to cause net interest payments to balloon to nearly $800 billion, or 3.4 percent of GDP, by 2020.

Many other outcomes are possible, however. If, for example, the tax reductions enacted earlier in the decade were continued, the alternative minimum tax was indexed for inflation, and future annual appropriations remained the same share of GDP that they were in 2010, debt held by the public would total nearly 100 percent of GDP by 2020. Interest costs would be correspondingly higher.

This CBO study describes historical trends in borrowing by the federal government and the interest the government pays on that borrowing. The study takes an in-depth look at the most commonly used measure of the government's debt—debt held by the public—and also discusses several other measures of the debt, such as debt held by the public net of financial assets, gross federal debt, and debt subject to limit. In addition, the study examines the government's net interest costs and the types of transactions that generate interest payments and collections.

Debt Held by the Public

To finance the government's activities, the Treasury issues numerous types of securities that vary in their maturity, how they are sold, and how their payments are structured. Marketable securities—bills, notes, bonds, and inflation-protected securities—are auctioned at regular intervals during the year and accounted for nearly 95 percent of outstanding debt held by the public at the end of 2010. Nearly two-thirds of that marketable debt was in Treasury notes, which have an original maturity of 2 to 10 years.

A small percentage of debt held by the public is in the form of nonmarketable securities, which cannot be resold by the original purchasers. Those securities include savings bonds, securities issued to state and local governments, and securities used for investments of the government's Thrift Savings Plan (a retirement savings program for civil service employees and members of the uniformed services).

The government's net borrowing for each year (that is, the new cash it must raise, over and above the amount required to pay off maturing securities) is determined largely by the size of the federal deficit. However, a number of other factors—collectively labeled "other means of financing" and not directly included in budget totals— also affect the amount of debt that the government issues. Those factors include changes in the government's cash balances and the cash flows of federal credit programs (mostly programs that provide loans and loan guarantees).

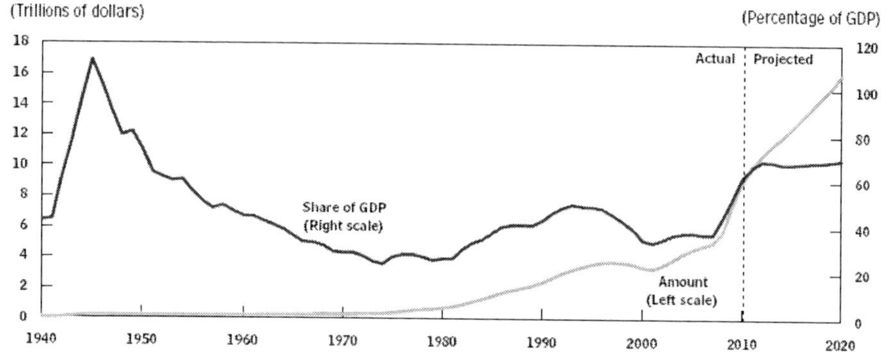

Sources: Congressional Budget Office; historical data are based on information from the Office of Management and Budget.

Note: GDP = gross domestic product.

Summary Figure 1. Debt Held by the Public, 1940 to 2020.

Many investors consider federal debt to be an attractive investment, in part because it is essentially free of any risk of default. At the end of 2010, domestic entities owned about 53 percent of the outstanding public debt, and foreign entities owned about 47 percent. Central banks and private entities in China, Japan, and the United Kingdom are the largest foreign investors.

Other Measures of Federal Debt

In addition to debt held by the public, a number of other measures of federal debt are used for various purposes. Debt held by the public net of financial assets is a measure that reflects the fact that the government affects financial markets not only by borrowing but also by acquiring financial assets. Those assets affect the government's financial condition: If sold, the proceeds could be used to pay down a portion of the federal debt; if retained by the government, they will generate inflows from interest, dividends, and repayments of principal that will reduce the government's future borrowing needs.

Debt held by the public net of financial assets is calculated by subtracting from debt held by the public the value of assets the government has acquired through its various activities in the credit markets (such as loans made by federal programs) and through its efforts to address the recent financial crisis (such as preferred stock in financial institutions), as well as its cash balances. At the end of 2010, debt net of financial assets totaled $8.0 trillion—$1.0

trillion less than debt held by the public and 55 percent of GDP (compared with 62 percent of GDP when financial assets are not taken into account). Debt held by the public net of financial assets provides a more comprehensive picture of the government's financial condition and its overall impact on credit markets than debt held by the public, but calculating it is not straightforward because neither the universe of such assets nor the method for valuing them is well defined.

Assessing the government's overall financial condition requires accounting not only for debt that the government has already incurred (and financial assets it has acquired) but also for commitments the government has made for the future. Debt held by the public, with or without an adjustment for the government's financial assets, does not account for such future obligations. One useful barometer of the future fiscal situation is projections of changes in debt held by the public relative to GDP; that measure indicates whether the government's participation in credit markets is expected to grow faster or slower than economic output. Another useful gauge is the fiscal gap, which measures the immediate change in spending or revenues that would be necessary to keep the projected debt-to-GDP ratio the same at the end of a given period as at the beginning of the period. The fiscal gap quantifies the projected long-term shortfall of revenues relative to outlays in present-value terms—that is, as a single number that describes a flow of future revenues or outlays in terms of an equivalent lump sum received or spent today. These forward-looking measures are not addressed in this study but are used extensively in other CBO publications.[2]

Gross debt, which comprises federal debt held by the public plus Treasury securities held by federal trust funds and other government accounts, is sometimes used to evaluate the government's overall fiscal situation. At the end of 2010, gross federal debt totaled $13.5 trillion— the $9.0 trillion in debt held by the public plus $4.5 trillion in debt held by government accounts. More than half of the latter amount is held by the Social Security trust funds. Because those trust funds and other government accounts are part of the federal government, transactions between them and the Treasury are intra-governmental; that is, the government securities in those funds are an asset to the individual programs but a liability to the rest of the government. The resources needed to redeem the government securities in the trust funds and other accounts in some future year must be generated from taxes, income from other government sources, or borrowing by the government in that year.

Gross debt is not a good indicator of the government's fiscal condition, however (nor is debt subject to limit, the amount of federal debt that is subject to the overall limit set in law and is roughly equal to gross debt). The value of Treasury securities held by trust funds and other government accounts measures only some of the commitments the government has made for the future, and it includes some amounts that may not represent future obligations at all. Moreover, because those securities represent internal transactions of the government, they have no direct effect on credit markets.

Interest Payments and Receipts

The government pays and collects interest in various ways. Its net interest outlays are equal to the interest it pays minus the interest it receives. Net interest outlays are dominated by the interest paid to holders of the debt that the Treasury issues to the public. Although the Treasury also issues debt to trust funds and other government accounts, the payment of interest to those accounts is an intragovernmental transaction that has no effect on net interest outlays or on the budget deficit.

The federal government's interest payments depend primarily on interest rates and the amount of debt held by the public. Other factors, such as the rate of inflation and the maturity structure of outstanding securities, also affect interest costs (for example, long-term bonds generally carry higher interest rates than do short-term bills). Interest rates are determined by a combination of market forces and the policies of the Federal Reserve. Debt held by the public is determined mostly by cumulative budget deficits, which depend on policy choices about spending and revenues and on economic conditions and other factors.

Although the federal government has increased its net borrowing by more than $3 trillion in the past two years, net interest costs dropped from $253 billion in 2008 to $197 billion in 2010 because of remarkably low interest rates (see Summary Figure 2). The amounts of net interest shown in the budget include interest paid on all Treasury securities ($413 billion in 2010), minus the portion of that interest that is received by trust funds ($186 billion in 2010) and the net amount of other interest received by the government ($30 billion in 2010). The last category consists primarily of net receipts to the Treasury from the financing accounts for federal loan programs (those accounts are not included in the federal budget).

In CBO's most recent projections, which assume that current laws remain the same, annual deficits decline from the $1.3 trillion recorded in 2010, but the cumulative deficit from 2011 through 2020 exceeds $6.2 trillion.

Borrowing to finance that deficit—in combination with an expected rise in interest rates—would lead to a fourfold increase in net interest payments over the next 10 years, from $197 billion in 2010 to $778 billion in 2020. As a percentage of GDP, net interest outlays would more than double during that period, rising from 1.4 percent to 3.4 percent.

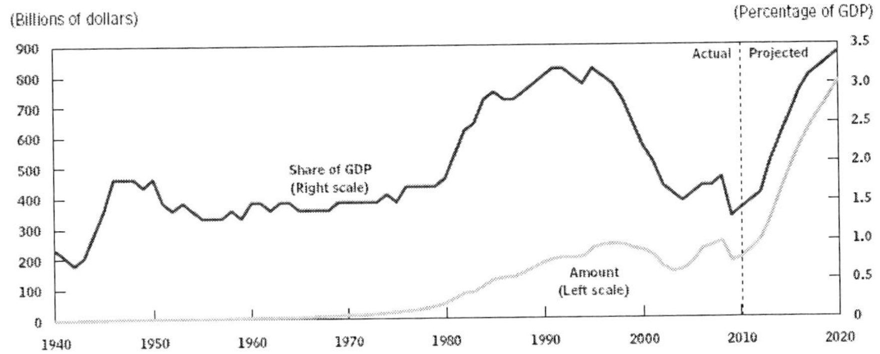

Sources: Congressional Budget Office; historical data are based on information from the Office of Management and Budget.

Note: GDP = gross domestic product.

Summary Figure 2. Net Interest Outlays, 1940 to 2020.

DEBT HELD BY THE PUBLIC

When the federal government's spending exceeds its revenues, which has been the case in all but 4 of the past 40 years, the Department of the Treasury must raise cash to finance the resulting budget deficit. It does so by selling securities in the capital markets. Debt held by the public consists almost entirely of those securities, including those sold to pay off securities as they mature.

Recently, the federal government has been recording the largest budget deficits, as a share of the economy, since the end of World War II. As a result of those deficits, the amount of federal debt held by the public has surged. At the end of 2008, that debt amounted to $5.8 trillion— equal to 40 percent of the nation's annual economic output (as measured by gross domestic product, or GDP), above the average over the previous 40 years of 35 percent. Since then, large budget deficits and increased borrowing to fund programs that address the recent financial crisis have caused debt held by the public to shoot upward, surpassing $9 trillion by the end of fiscal year 2010—equal to 62 percent of GDP, the highest percentage since shortly after World War II (see Figure 1-1 on page 4). The sharp rise in debt stems partly from lower tax revenues and higher federal spending related to the recent severe recession and turmoil in financial markets. However, the growing debt also reflects an imbalance between spending and revenues that predated those economic developments.

To finance the government's activities, the Treasury issues numerous types of securities that vary in their maturity, how they are sold, and how their interest payments are structured. Those differences directly affect the interest rates on those securities, which are a key determinant of the amount of interest the government pays on its outstanding debt.

The size of the federal deficit largely determines the government's net borrowing for each year (that is, the new cash it must raise, above the amount required to pay off maturing securities). However, several other factors—collectively labeled "other means of financing" and not directly included in budget totals—also affect the amount of debt that the government issues each year. Those factors include changes in the government's cash balances and the cash flows of federal credit programs, mostly programs that provide loans and loan guarantees. Also, a small amount of debt held by the public (less than 1 percent) is issued by agencies other than the Treasury (such as the Tennessee Valley Authority). Debt issued by Fannie Mae and Freddie Mac—the two government-sponsored enterprises now under federal conservatorship—is not included in debt held by the public (see Box 1-1).

Publicly issued Treasury securities are held by various buyers in the United States, including the Federal Reserve, private investors, and state and local governments. Those securities also are acquired by foreign investors, including foreign central banks and individuals.

Compared with a similar measure of debt held by the public, the amount of debt in the United States is substantially lower than that in Japan and Italy and close to that in Hungary and Portugal.

Trends in Debt Held by the Public

During World War II, the federal government borrowed heavily to finance the war effort and, as a result, debt reached 109 percent of GDP in 1946. For the next quarter century, however, debt hardly grew—inching up, by an average of about $2 billion a year, from $242 billion in 1946 to $283 billion in

1970. During that period, on balance, the government neither paid off the debt incurred from the war nor added much to it. With the economy growing, debt dropped steadily as a share of GDP, reaching 28 percent in 1970 (see Figure 1-1).

Box 1-1.
Accounting for Debt and Guarantees Issued by Fannie Mae and Freddie Mac

In September 2008, the Director of the Federal Housing Finance Agency placed into conservatorship two large government-sponsored enterprises, Fannie Mae and Freddie Mac.1 At the same time, the Secretary of the Treasury took a major ownership interest in both entities in the form of preferred stock. In the judgment of the Congressional Budget Office (CBO), those actions make Fannie Mae and Freddie Mac part of the government and imply that their operations should be reflected in the federal budget.2

Fannie Mae and Freddie Mac were chartered by the Congress four decades ago as private companies with a public mission to provide liquidity and stability to the secondary market for residential mortgages (the market in which those mortgages are bought and sold). In carrying out their charters, the two entities purchase mortgage loans made by lenders and package them into mortgage-backed securities (MBSs) that carry guarantees that principal and interest on the underlying mortgages will be paid in full; those securities are then sold to investors. The two entities also invest directly in mortgages and MBSs, which they hold in their portfolios. To fund those holdings, they issue debt and sell it in the international capital markets. As of September 2010, Fannie Mae and Freddie Mac held or guaranteed about $4.4 trillion in MBSs; they also had issued $1.6 trillion in debt.

Despite having a unique legal status and a long history linking them closely to the federal government, Fannie Mae and Freddie Mac had been considered private firms owned by their shareholders. Now, however, the federal government controls both entities and is operating them to fulfill the public purpose of supporting the housing and mortgage markets.3

Moreover, both entities rely on federal backing to maintain their low-cost access to financial markets. Although they are not legally government agencies and their employees are not civil servants, CBO believes it is appropriate and useful to policymakers to include Fannie Mae's and Freddie Mac's financial transactions with other federal activities in the budget.4

That budgetary treatment raises the question of how the conservatorship of Fannie Mae and Freddie Mac should be reflected in measures of the government's financial position. Neither CBO nor the Administration currently incorporates debt or MBSs issued by Fannie Mae and Freddie Mac in estimates of federal debt held by the public, nor does CBO currently include the value of the preferred shares held by the Department of the Treasury in its estimate of the value of financial assets owned by the government.

In taking over Fannie Mae and Freddie Mac, the government obtained both assets and liabilities. The assets consist mostly of the mortgages and MBSs held in the entities' portfolios and the claim to the revenue stream generated by guarantee fees. The liabilities consist mostly of debt issued by Fannie Mae and Freddie Mac and the obligation to honor their guarantees. In CBO's judgment, the liabilities are larger, on balance, than the assets because of elevated losses from defaults. Consequently, the two entities do not represent a net asset to the government but a net liability— that is, their impact on the government's financial position is a negative one. CBO estimated the amount of that negative impact when the entities were taken into conservatorship, but it has not updated that estimate nor included such an amount in debt held by the public or any other measures of debt referenced in this study.

1. Conservatorship is the legal process by which an entity (in this case, the government) establishes control and oversight of a company to put it in a sound and solvent condition.
2. See Congressional Budget Office, *CBO's Budgetary Treatment of Fannie Mae and Freddie Mac*, Background Paper (January 2010).
3. For more information about the various ways in which the federal government helps the housing market, see Congressional Budget Office, *An Overview of Federal Support for Housing*, Issue Brief (November 2009).
4. The Administration's Office of Management and Budget (OMB) makes the ultimate decision about whether the activities of Fannie Mae and Freddie Mac will be included in the federal budget. Although OMB's budget documents have not included those activities in the budget totals, they have provided financial information about the two entities for several years; see, for example, *Budget of the United States Government, Fiscal Year 2011: Appendix*, pp. 1373–1375.

The era of slow growth of debt ended in the 1970s. Federal budgets were unbalanced for the entire decade, and debt held by the public more than doubled in dollar terms between 1970 and 1980. But rapid inflation swelled GDP, and the debt as a percentage of GDP actually decreased somewhat during the decade, falling to 26 percent by 1980.

Between 1980 and 1993, debt held by the public expanded more rapidly than the economy, rising from 26 percent of GDP to 49 percent. However, policies adopted during the 1990s to tackle budget deficits, and the surge in tax revenues associated with robust economic growth seen throughout most of the decade, led to budget surpluses between 1998 and 2001. Those surpluses decreased debt held by the public by more than $450 billion between the end of 1997 and the end of 2001 and lowered debt as a share of GDP to 33 percent by the end of 2001, a level not seen since the early 1980s. Those surpluses were short-lived, though, as budget deficits between 2002 and 2007 boosted debt held by the public by more than $1.7 trillion, but economic growth kept debt as a percentage of GDP fairly steady in that period, around 37 percent.

In 2008, the United States experienced the most severe financial crisis since the Great Depression. The following year, revenues dropped sharply and outlays increased substantially, pushing the deficit to $1.4 trillion, equal to 10 percent of GDP (the highest level since 1945). The budget deficit in 2010 reached nearly $1.3 trillion (or 9 percent of GDP) because of continued low revenues and elevated spending. Overall, in the three years between 2008 and 2010, the Treasury added nearly $4 trillion to its borrowing, increasing debt held by the public as a percentage of GDP from 36 percent at the end of 2007 to 40 percent at the end of 2008 and to 62 percent at the end of 2010.

Types and Amounts of Treasury Debt Held by the Public

The Treasury issues two broad types of securities to the public: marketable and nonmarketable. Marketable issues—bills, notes, bonds, and inflation-protected securities—are auctioned at regular intervals during the year and can be resold on the secondary market (where previously issued Treasury securities can be bought and resold). Such securities accounted for $8.5 trillion, or 94 percent, of debt held by the public at the end of 2010. Nonmarketable issues, such as savings bonds, are not sold at auction and cannot be traded in the secondary market. Those issues accounted for $526 billion, or 6 percent, of debt held by the public at the end of 2010 (see Figure 1-2).

Marketable Securities

Marketable securities comprise bills (original maturity of 1 year or less), notes (original maturity of 2 to 10 years), bonds (original maturity of longer than 10 years), and Treasury inflation-protected securities, or TIPS (original maturity of 5, 10, or 30 years). Bills are offered on a discount basis—that is, the purchaser generally pays less than the face value for a security and receives the face value at maturity; the difference between the purchase price and the value at maturity is the amount of interest earned on the security. In contrast, notes and bonds are referred to as "coupon" securities; the purchaser receives semiannual interest payments (the coupon) based on a fixed rate and receives the principal at maturity. TIPS provide purchasers with an inflation adjustment to the principal and a semiannual interest payment.[3] The interest rate on TIPS is a fixed rate determined at auction, but the interest payments vary because the rate is applied to the inflation-adjusted principal. TIPS mitigate the risk to investors that inflation will turn out to be higher than expected and tend to attract a somewhat different type of investor than those interested in other types of Treasury securities.

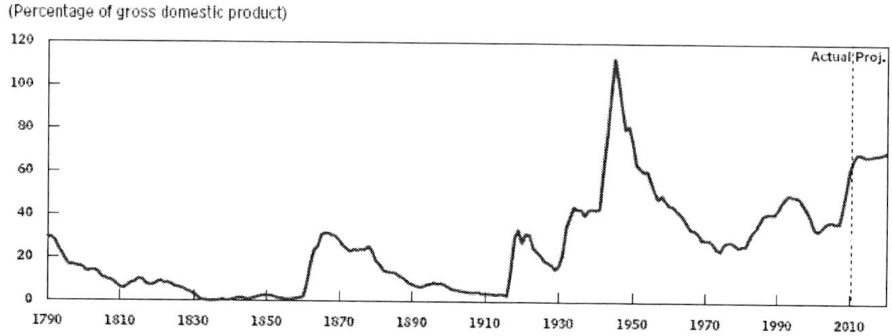

Sources: Congressional Budget Office based on data on federal debt from the Department of the Treasury and the Board of Governors of the Federal Reserve System. Estimates of gross domestic product come from the U.S. Census Bureau; Thomas Berry, *Revised Annual Estimates of American Gross National Product* (Richmond, Va.: Bostwick Press, 1978); Robert E. Gallman, "Economic Growth and Structural Change in the Long Nineteenth Century," in Gallman and Stanley L. Engerman, eds., *The Cambridge Economic History of the United States*, vol. 2, *The Long Nineteenth Century* (Cambridge, England: Cambridge University Press, 2000), pp. 1–55; Nathan S. Balke and Robert J. Gordon, "The Estimation of Prewar Gross National Product: Methodology and New Evidence," *Journal of Political Economy*, vol. 97, no. 1 (February 1989), pp. 38–92; and the Department of Commerce, Bureau of Economic Analysis.

Figure 1-1. Debt Held by the Public, 1790 to 2020.

Over the past two decades, Treasury notes have generally accounted for the majority of outstanding marketable securities; the current share of 62 percent is the highest since 1997 (see Figure 1-3; also see Table A-1 in the appendix for amounts outstanding for each type of security for the past 20 years). Bills have generally accounted for between 20 percent and 30 percent of marketable debt; the current share is at the lower end of that range. Bonds now account for 10 percent of outstanding marketable debt, about half of their share in the 1990s and early 2000s. The share in the form of TIPS increased over the 10 years from their inception to 2007; that share peaked at 10 percent of outstanding marketable securities but has fallen over the past three years.

In choosing the mix of maturities to offer, the Treasury must weigh several considerations. Short-term securities generally have lower interest costs, but they also incur the cost of more frequent refinancing, and they expose the government to the risk of having to pay higher interest rates when it refinances those issues. Conversely, longterm securities involve higher rates, on average, but provide more certainty about future costs of interest payments and reduce the frequency of refinancing. The preferences of investors are a further consideration in setting the maturity structure; offerings that best meet the needs of investors will lower the Treasury's overall cost of borrowing.

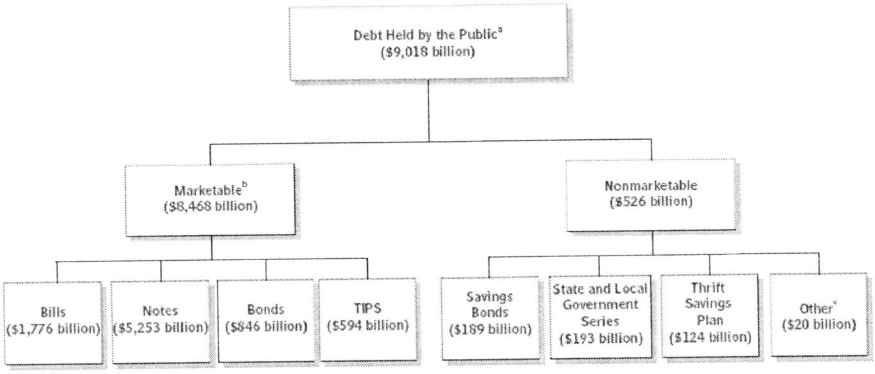

Figure 1-2. Components of Debt Held by the Public at the End of Fiscal Year 2010.

Auctions

The Treasury sells securities on a regular basis through "single-price" auctions, in which successful bidders buy securities at the highest accepted discount rate (for bills) or yield (for notes and bonds). Bidding can be either competitive or noncompetitive. Most competitive bidding is done by large financial institutions for their own accounts or on behalf of customers in the secondary (resale) market. Investors make a competitive bid by specifying the price they are willing to pay for a particular security at auction, but such bids are not guaranteed to be accepted.

Noncompetitive bids are made by investors through the Treasury or through certain banks, brokers, or dealers. Noncompetitive buyers specify an amount to purchase before an auction but are not allowed to specify a yield; instead, their bid is guaranteed to be fulfilled at the highest accepted yield.

Those buyers are assured of receiving the full amount of their order up to the current maximum of $5 million.

Borrowing Schedule

Treasury securities are issued on a regular schedule, and the amount to be auctioned is determined by the federal government's borrowing needs. The auction schedule and the mix of maturities are also designed to enhance the liquidity of Treasury issues so that investors can buy or sell them quickly and in large amounts without affecting the price of the securities. Treasury issues that are relatively liquid are more valuable to most investors, who are therefore willing to pay more for them.

With the rapid increase in the deficit over the past few years, the auction schedule has been expanded. In particular, the Treasury has increased the number of auctions, raised the dollar amount of individual issuances, and reintroduced a variety of previously retired maturities (see Table 1-1 for the Treasury's recent auction schedule). Most of the recent borrowing has been done in securities with a maturity of greater than a year, which has allowed the Treasury to lock in historically low rates on those securities.

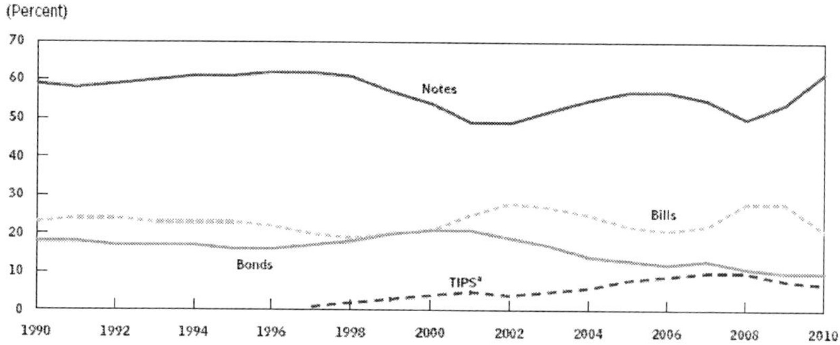

Source: Congressional Budget Office based on data from the Department of the Treasury.

a. Treasury inflation-protected securities (TIPS) were first issued in 1997.

Figure 1-3. Percentage of Marketable Debt Outstanding, by Type of Security, 1990 to 2010.

Bills

The Treasury offers bills in 1-month, 3-month, and 6-month maturities on a weekly basis. It also offers a 1-year bill every four weeks; that issue, which had not been offered since 2001, was reintroduced in 2008. The Treasury also offers cash management bills (CMBs) to fund the government's short-term cash needs; CMBs have no uniform maturity date and are offered as needed. At the end of fiscal year 2010, the outstanding face value of Treasury bills totaled roughly $1.8 trillion, representing about 21 percent of all marketable Treasury debt.

Notes

The Treasury's portfolio of notes has changed significantly over the past decade. At the beginning of 2000, following a string of annual surpluses, notes were offered only in maturities of 2, 5, and 10 years. In 2003, after two years of deficits, the 3-year note was reintroduced; in 2008, with debt continuing to grow, the Treasury reintroduced the 7-year note. Notes are currently offered monthly in maturities of 2, 3, 5, and 7 years, and quarterly in a maturity of 10 years. In the months between the quarterly auctions, the 10-year notes are sold in a ccreopening."[4] At the end of 2010, the outstanding value of notes was roughly $5.3 trillion, accounting for about 62 percent of all marketable debt.

Bonds

The Treasury temporarily stopped issuing bonds in 2001 in light of the improvement in the budget balance over the previous few years. That hiatus was short-lived, however, and in 2006 the Treasury announced that it would again offer 30-year bonds. Such bonds are now issued quarterly, with interim reopenings on a monthly basis. At the end of 2010, $846 billion in bonds was outstanding, representing about 10 percent of all marketable debt.

Treasury Inflation-Protected Securities

In 1997, the Treasury added TIPS to its auction schedule, beginning with-maturities of 10 and 30 years. It discontinued issuing 30-year TIPS in 2001, began issuing TIPS with maturities of 5 and 20 years in 2004, but reverted to issuing 30-year TIPS in lieu of the 20-year security in 2010.

Outstanding TIPS totaled $594 billion at the end of 2010, or about 7 percent of all marketable debt.

Table 1-1. Schedule of Treasury Auctions of Marketable Debt

Type of Issue and Maturity	Issues per Year	Timing of Auctions	Size of Recent Auctions (Billions of dollars)
Bills			
One month (28 days)	52	Weekly	34 a

Table 1-1. (Continued)

Type of Issue and Maturity	Issues per Year	Timing of Auctions	Size of Recent Auctions (Billions of dollars)
Three months (91 days)	52	Weekly	29 a
Six months (182 days)	52	Weekly	29 a
One year (364 days)	13	Every four weeks	25
Cash management	Variable	As needed	Variable
Notes			
Two years	12	Monthly	37
Three years	12	Monthly	33
Five years	12	Monthly	36
Seven years	12	Monthly	30
Ten years	12	Quarterly, with interim reopenings	25 b
Bonds (Thirty years)	12	Quarterly, with interim reopenings	17 c
Treasury Inflation-Protected			
Securities			
Five years	2	Annually, with an interim reopening	11 d
Ten years	6	Semiannually, with interim reopenings	12 e
Thirty years	2	Annually, with an interim reopening	8 f

Source: Congressional Budget Office based on data from the Department of the Treasury.

Note: In a reopening, the Treasury issues an additional amount of a previously issued security. The reopened security has the same maturity date and interest rate as the original security but has a different issue date and, usually, a different purchase price.

a The average amount issued in September 2010.

b Interim reopenings were $21 billion each.

c Interim reopenings were $13 billion each.

d Interim reopening was $10 billion.

e Interim reopenings were $10 billion each.

f Interim reopening was $7 billion.

Maturity

The average remaining maturity of outstanding marketable securities has fluctuated over the past decade, from a high of almost 6 years at the end of 2000 to a low of close to 4 years in 2008 (Figure 1-4). Increased borrowing in notes and bonds raised the average maturity of outstanding debt to nearly 5 years at the end of 2010.

Seasonality

Federal borrowing has a pronounced seasonal pattern and is typically highest in the second quarter of the fiscal year (January through March) and lowest in the third quarter (April through June), coinciding with the April deadline for filing individual income tax returns. That pattern is sometimes obscured by changes in fiscal policy and fluctuations in economic conditions; it can also be affected if the Congress fails to approve a higher debt ceiling sufficiently in advance to avoid disrupting Treasury auctions. (The debt ceiling is described in Chapter 2.)

Seasonal fluctuations in borrowing are more pronounced for Treasury bills than they are for notes and bonds (see Figure 1-5). Because bills are issued more frequently and have shorter maturities, the Treasury can quickly adjust the size of such auctions in response to fluctuations in the government's funding requirements. issuance of bills (the amount of new issuances minus the amount of maturing bills) varies greatly from quarter to quarter. Including cash management bills, the net quarterly issuance of bills during the past five years has ranged from a net paydown of almost $200 billion to a net issuance of roughly $430 billion.

Nonmarketable Securities

Nonmarketable securities are nontransferable debt instruments that are not traded in secondary markets. Savings bonds and securities issued to the federal government's Thrift Savings Plan (TSP) and to state and local governments account for most of the outstanding nonmarketable securities; foreign and domestic zero-coupon bonds and other issues account for a much smaller portion.[5] Unlike the issuance of marketable securities, which is directly tied to the size of the federal deficit, the issuance of nonmarketable securities depends on the demand for them by investors. From 2000 to 2001, for example, the government experienced a budget surplus, yet non-marketable debt grew from $374 billion to $386 billion. Outstanding nonmarketable debt totaled $526 billion at the end of 2010 (see Figure 1-2 on page 5; also see Table A-2 in the appendix for amounts outstanding for each type of security for the past 20 years).

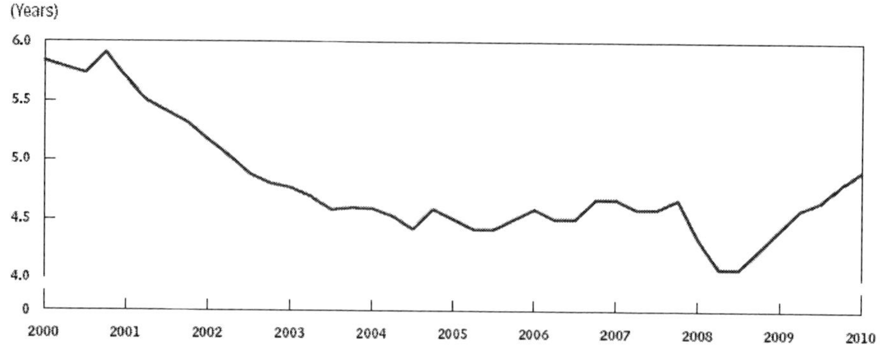

Source: Congressional Budget Office based on data from the Department of the Treasury.

Figure 1-4. Average Remaining Maturity of Marketable Public Debt, 2000 to 2010.

Savings Bonds

Savings bonds originated in 1935 but became popular during World War II as a means of helping to finance the war effort. Formerly purchased out of a sense of patriotism, savings bonds are now generally purchased as gifts or through payroll deductions by individual investors; they come in several series with varying characteristics.[6] The amount of outstanding savings bonds totaled almost $190 billion at the end of 2010.

EE/E Bonds

EE bonds are currently offered as coupon securities (if purchased electronically) and on a discount basis (if a paper version is purchased). Bonds sold as a coupon security accumulate interest in monthly installments and can earn interest for up to 30 years. Those sold as a discount security are purchased at half of their face value and are paid in full at maturity. The face value of outstanding EE bonds (and E bonds, their predecessors) totaled about $122 billion at the end of 2010.

Other Types of Savings Bonds

The Treasury also issues inflation-indexed savings bonds, known as the I series; about $41 billion in I bonds was outstanding at the end of 2010. The HH/H series, which was discontinued in 2004, makes coupon payments to bond holders every six months; the face value of outstanding HH/H bonds totaled $9 billion at the end of 2010. Individual investors also hold savings bonds that have matured but have not been redeemed; those securities do not accrue any additional interest. The outstanding amount of such bonds was about $16 billion at the end of 2010 (savings bonds that have matured are not included in the amounts listed for the various types of savings bonds).

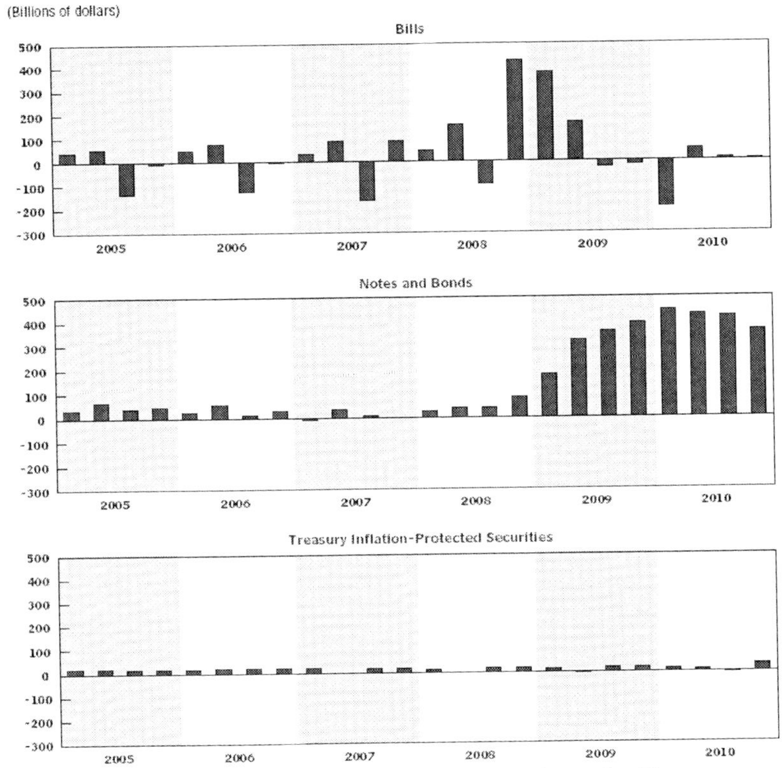

Source: Congressional Budget Office based on data from the Department of the Treasury.

Figure 1-5. Quarterly Change in Outstanding Treasury Securities, 2005 to 2010.

State and Local Government Series

The Treasury offers state and local government series (SLGS) securities as part of its regulation of the tax-exemption privilege accorded to such governments. States and municipalities may issue tax-exempt bonds, which typically carry interest rates below those of taxable instruments, such as marketable Treasury securities or corporate bonds. In the absence of rules to the contrary, issuers of those tax-exempt bonds would have an incentive to borrow at tax-exempt rates and reinvest the funds at higher, taxable rates, thereby making a profit. To bar that practice, known as tax arbitrage, federal law allows state and local governments to borrow only for legitimate public purposes (to build infrastructure, for example). However, funds that are borrowed for such purposes might sit idle for some time (before construction of infrastructure begins, say), so issuers are allowed to invest the funds in SLGS securities for that period without violating the ban on arbitrage. SLGS securities carry an interest rate of one basis point (one one-hundredth of a percentage point) below a Treasury security with a similar maturity. The Treasury also offers state and local governments the opportunity to place their funds in demand deposit accounts with the Treasury; interest accrues on those deposits each day, with the rate keyed to the yield in the most recent auction of the 3-month Treasury bill.[7]

Because of increased financial strain at the state and local level in recent years, demand for SLGS securities has declined substantially. In 2007, the face value of outstanding SLGS securities reached a peak of nearly $300 billion. By the end of 2010, their value had fallen to just over $190 billion, a 35 percent decrease since 2007.

Thrift Savings Plan

The TSP is a retirement savings program for civil service employees and members of the uniformed services. The TSP is designed to be similar to 401(k) plans found in the private sector by providing federal employees with opportunities to invest in funds that track different sorts of financial assets, including domestic and foreign equities, fixed-income securities, and U.S. government securities. Those government securities are nonmarketable Treasury securities issued specifically to the TSP. They have short maturities but earn a long-term interest rate equal to the weighted average market yield on outstanding marketable Treasury securities with 4 or more years to maturity. In total, the value of those securities was $124 billion at the end of 2010.

Zero-Coupon Bonds and Other Nonmarketable Securities

The government issued zero-coupon bonds with a face value of $30 billion to the Resolution Funding Corporation, a government-sponsored enterprise, as part of a plan to resolve the savings and loan crisis of the 1980s. The outstanding value of that issuance at the end of 2010 was $11 billion. The government also issued $14 billion in zero-coupon bonds to Argentina and Venezuela in the late 1980s to help ease their debt burden; less than $2 billion remained outstanding at the end of 2010. (The Treasury issued more than $30 billion in such bonds to Mexico; those bonds have already been paid off.)

Table 1-2. Deficits and Means of Financing, 2000 to 2010

	2000	2001	2002	2003	2004	2005	2006	2007	2008	2009	2010
Surplus or Deficit (-)	236	128	-158	-378	-413	-318	-248	-161	-459	-1,413	-1,294
Other means of financing											
Changes to the Treasury's cash balancea	4	8	-17	26	-1	1	-16	-23	-296	96	-35
Otherb	-17	-46	-46	-21	32	21	28	-22	-13	-425	-145
Subtotal	-14	-38	-63	5	31	22	11	-45	-309	-329	-180
from the Publicc Net Treasury Borrowing	223	90	-221	-373	-382	-297	-237	-206	-768	-1,742	-1,474

In addition, the federal government has numerous other small accounts with nonmarketable securities that totaled $7 billion in 2010. The total value of zero-coupon bonds and other nonmarketable securities was $20 billion at the end of 2010.

Reasons for Borrowing Other than Budget Deficits

The amount the Treasury borrows or redeems is determined primarily by the budget deficit or surplus in a given year. However, other factors, collectively referred to as "other means of financing," also affect the government's need to borrow from the public. Before the recent financial crisis, those other factors had a relatively small effect on total borrowing—ranging, between 2000 and 2007, from a reduction of about $40 billion to an increase of roughly $60 billion. The effects on borrowing arose mostly from changes in the Treasury's cash balances and from the differences between the cash flows associated with federal credit programs and the costs of those programs on a present-value basis, which is how they are recorded in the budget.[8] However, borrowing for reasons other than budget deficits rose sharply in 2008 and 2009 as a result of policies enacted during the financial crisis; specifically, additional borrowing by the Treasury totaled more than $300 billion each year for programs such as the Troubled Asset Relief Program (TARP) and the Supplementary Financing Program (SFP), which are discussed below. In 2010, the amount of borrowing for reasons other than the budget deficit totaled $180 billion, mainly to fund lending to students (see Table 1-2).

Credit Programs

The federal budget does not record the cash flows of federal credit programs; instead, it recognizes the net subsidy costs associated with such activities.[9] Subsidy costs are the expected lifetime cost to the government of a loan, loan guarantee, or asset purchase and are recorded in the budget when the transaction occurs. That treatment results in a disconnect between the budget and the Treasury's borrowing, because the Treasury's borrowing needs are determined by the cash flows of the transactions. For loans made directly by the government, for example, the amount the government must borrow is generally greater than the cost recorded in the budget; for a loan program with a 10 percent subsidy rate, the government might disburse $1,000 in cash for a loan and then receive cash repayments later, but the budget would record a

$100 cost in the year of disbursement and nothing in future years (unless the estimated subsidy rate turned out to be incorrect).

To reconcile those transactions, the government uses "credit financing accounts," which are not part of the budget. Those accounts are credited with the program's subsidy payments (that is, the subsidy amounts shown in the budget) and record all the cash flows associated with the program. If the financing accounts need up-front cash (for example, to cover disbursements on direct loans), those funds are borrowed from the Treasury, which in turn borrows them from the public.

Before the recent financial crisis, net cash flows through the financing accounts were relatively small and driven mainly by student loan programs. In 2009, net cash disbursements from the financing accounts increased substantially, exceeding $400 billion, mainly because of the TARP and the Treasury's purchases of mortgage-backed securities (MBSs).[10] Net cash disbursements in 2010 dropped to just over $150 billion, mostly for student loans (partially offset by repayments and dividends from recipients of TARP funds).

As of November 2010, three programs accounted for the vast majority of the outstanding debt used to finance government credit programs: student loans, the TARP, and purchases of MBSs by the Treasury.

Student Loans

The student loan program is the largest direct loan program administered by the federal government. Until recently, the Department of Education provided direct loans to students and also guaranteed loans made to students by lenders in the private sector. In March 2010, the Health Care and Education Reconciliation Act of 2010 (Public Law 111-152) eliminated the program that provided federal guarantees for student loans, replacing future guarantees with direct loans made by the federal government.

The Treasury's net borrowing needs for student loans are driven by the up-front disbursements and periodic repayments that are recorded in the financing accounts. The Congressional Budget Office (CBO) estimates that in 2011—the first full year in which direct loans are the only type being made—the Treasury's net disbursements (total disbursements minus collections from existing loans) will exceed the subsidy cost recorded in the budget by $112 billion. More broadly, the shift to direct loans will increase the Treasury's borrowing needs in the next several years as the loans are disbursed, but it will decrease net borrowing in later years as borrowers repay the interest and principal. Part of the additional borrowing also stems from defaults on outstanding guaranteed loans. CBO estimates that those guarantees will cost roughly $10 billion annually over the next 10 years.

Troubled Asset Relief Program

The Emergency Economic Stabilization Act of 2008 (Division A of P.L. 110-343) created a program, known as the TARP, to promote stability in financial markets by purchasing or guaranteeing up to $700 billion in "troubled assets."[11] The Treasury made large cash outlays to fund investments in financial institutions and certain other firms, and the estimated subsidy costs of those transactions were recorded in the budget. Therefore, the Treasury's net borrowing needs at the outset of the program were significantly greater than the costs recorded in the budget. As of November 18, 2010, the Treasury had disbursed $389 billion to TARP participants, and $166 billion of that funding remained outstanding. Future dividend and interest payments to the Treasury and the proceeds from the sale of its investments in preferred stock are expected to reduce the Treasury's borrowing needs over the next several years. (CBO now estimates that the net cost of the program will be about $25 billion.)

Purchases of Mortgage-Backed Securities

In September 2008, the Treasury announced that it would purchase MBSs from private holders to promote stability in the mortgage market and lessen upward pressure on mortgage rates. The Treasury needed to borrow to finance the initial purchases of such securities, and it will receive cash payments of interest and principal while holding those securities; at the time of the purchase, however, the budget reflected only the estimated net earnings (which were subsequently updated and now total about $14 billion on a present-value basis) over the life of the program. In 2008 and 2009, the Treasury made net disbursements of $5 billion and $171 billion, respectively, for the MBS program. In 2010, net inflows related to MBS purchases yielded more than $3 billion in cash to the Treasury. CBO projects annual cash inflows of about $9 billion per year through 2020.

Supplementary Financing Program

The SFP was established in September 2008 to help the Federal Reserve conduct monetary policy and stabilize the financial system during the financial crisis.[12] The Treasury auctioned CMBs as part of its normal operations and placed the cash raised into an account at the Federal Reserve. That account held more than $550 billion in cash at its peak in November 2008, but the balance had dropped to about $200 billion by the end of 2010. The deposits that built up the SFP account added to the Treasury's borrowing requirements at the time, but the decline in the balance has reduced those requirements more recently; none of those cash flows affected the budget deficit. CBO anticipates that the SFP will be phased out in 2011.

Table 1-3. Holders of Public Debt at the End of Fiscal Years 2005 and 2010

	2005		2010	
Domestic Holders	Billions of Dollars	Percentage of Total	Billions of Dollars	Percentage of Total
Individuals	501	10.9	1,083	12.0
Federal Reserve	736	16.0	812	9.0
Pension and retirement funds	311	6.8	775	8.6
Mutual funds	238	5.2	603	6.7
State and local governments	448	9.8	509	5.6
Other	367	8.0	977	10.8
Subtotal	2,602	56.7	4,759	52.8
Foreign Holders[a]				
China	306	6.7	884	9.8
Japan	673	14.7	865	9.6
United Kingdom	96	2.1	459	5.1
Domestic Holders	Billions of Dollars	Percentage of Total	Billions of Dollars	Percentage of Total
Oil exporters[b]	66	1.4	231	2.6
Brazil	28	0.6	165	1.8
Other	822	17.9	1,656	18.4
Subtotal	1,990	43.3	4,259	47.2
Total	4,592	100.0	9,018	100.0

Source: Congressional Budget Office based on Board of Governors of the Federal Reserve System, Flow of Funds Accounts of the United States: Flows and Outstandings, December 9, 2010 (for domestic holders and total foreign holders), and Treasury International Capital Survey, November 16, 2010 (for individual foreign countries).

a. Data for foreign countries include holdings by individuals, businesses, and government entities. Data for individual foreign countries were estimated by the Federal Reserve on the basis of its survey of holdings.

b. Includes Algeria, Bahrain, Ecuador, Gabon, Indonesia, Iran, Iraq, Kuwait, Libya, Nigeria, Oman, Qatar, Saudi Arabia, the United Arab Emirates, and Venezuela.

Other Factors Affecting the Treasury's Borrowing

A few government agencies other than the Treasury issue their own debt; the Tennessee Valley Authority accounts for almost all of the $24 billion in non-Treasury debt included in debt held by the public at the end of 2010.[13] Agencies' borrowing affects the Treasury's borrowing needs; all other things being equal, if agencies can borrow on their own behalf, then the Treasury does not need to do so. Other factors that the Treasury weighs when deciding how much to borrow include reductions (or increases) in its cash balances, changes in the amount of checks outstanding, and changes in accrued interest costs that are included in budget outlays but have not yet been paid.[14]

Ownership of Federal Debt Held by the Public

Investors consider federal debt to be an attractive investment because they view it as being essentially free of any risk of default. Treasury securities also are valued for their liquidity—they can be bought and sold quickly and in large quantities without affecting their price. Domestic investors owned about $4.8 trillion of debt held by the public outstanding at the end of 2010, and foreign investors owned about $4.3 trillion (see Table 1-3).

Domestic Ownership

Domestic holdings of U.S. public debt have increased substantially in the past five years, from about $2.6 trillion in 2005 to $4.8 trillion in 2010. Individuals, including personal trusts and estates, own almost $1.1 trillion in Treasury securities, about 12 percent of the total.

A significant amount of federal debt is held by the Federal Reserve—the nation's central bank and an independent entity within the government that is responsible for conducting monetary policy, among other activities. The Federal Reserve typically has implemented monetary policy by buying and selling securities issued by the Treasury in the open market (or by borrowing or lending with such securities as collateral).[15] When the Federal Reserve wants to lower interest rates, it purchases Treasury securities (or lends funds with Treasury securities as collateral), which raises the amount of funds available to banks for lending. Conversely, when the Federal Reserve wants to raise interest rates, it sells some of its holdings of securities (or borrows funds with such securities as collateral). At the end of 2010, the Federal Reserve held $812 billion in outstanding Treasury securities, accounting for about 9 percent of debt held by the public. In 2005, it held $736 billion—a slightly smaller amount than in 2010 but a substantially higher percentage of the total (16 percent).

Other major holders of debt include pension and retirement funds, mutual funds, and state and local governments. Mutual funds' holdings have grown the most rapidly of that group over the past five years, more than doubling from $238 billion in 2005 to $603 billion in 2010. Pension funds also boosted their holdings of Treasury securities, from $311 billion to $775 billion over the same period. State and local governments increased their holdings from $448 billion to $509 billion.

Foreign Ownership

Foreign holdings of U.S. debt also have increased substantially in the past five years, from about $2.0 trillion in 2005 to $4.3 trillion in 2010. As a percentage of debt held by the public, foreign holdings have edged up, from about 43 percent to about 47 percent, during that period. Overall, the central banks and private entities in China, Japan, and the United Kingdom are the largest foreign investors, holding more than $2.2 trillion in Treasury securities, or nearly 25 percent of outstanding debt held by the public. Investors in China now hold significantly more debt than in earlier years, and the share of debt held by entities in Japan has declined noticeably. (Information about foreign holders of Treasury debt should be viewed as approximate. In many cases, it is impossible to accurately determine the home country of a foreign holder of U.S. securities because intermediaries may be involved in the custody, management, purchase, or sale of the securities.)

U.S. Debt Compared with that of Other Countries

Currently, no measure of debt for other countries completely mirrors U.S. debt held by the public. However, a calculation by the Organisation for Economic Cooperation and Development (OECD) of general government debt net of financial liabilities, although not a perfect equivalent to U.S. debt held by the public, historically has been similar to that measure.[16] Among the 33 OECD member countries, the 10 countries with the largest debt as a percentage of GDP had debt at the end of calendar year 2009 that ranged from about 40 percent of GDP for Iceland to more than 100 percent for Japan (see Figure 1-6). By comparison, the U.S. debt, as reported by the OECD, was 60 percent of GDP at the end of calendar year 2009—similar to that found in Hungary and Portugal.[17]

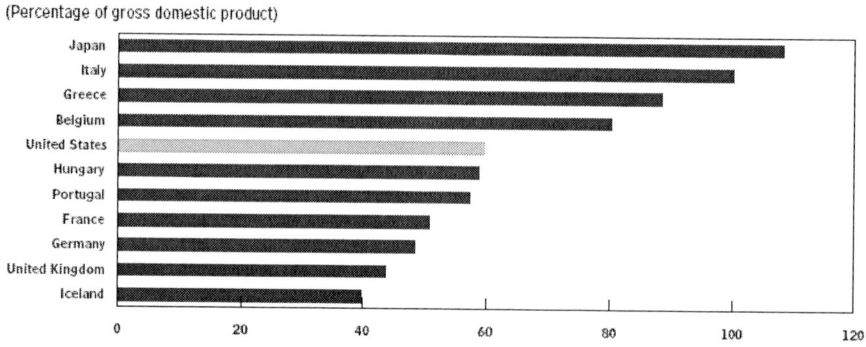

Source: Congressional Budget Office based on data from the Organisation for Economic Co-operation and Development.

Figure 1-6. Debt of Selected Countries at the End of Calendar Year 2009.

At the end of 2000, the U.S. debt—as calculated by the OECD—was equal to 35 percent of GDP, about 25 percentage points lower than in 2009. The increase in U.S. debt relative to GDP between 2000 and 2009 is larger than the growth seen in the United Kingdom (17 percentage points of GDP), France (16 percentage points), or Germany (14 percentage points) but smaller than increases in Japan (48 percentage points) and Portugal (30 percentage points).

Other Measures of Federal Debt

A number of other measures of federal debt are used for various purposes. Two important purposes are to assess the impact of borrowing by the federal government on financial markets and to assess the government's overall financial condition.

Regarding the first purpose, assessing the impact of the government's borrowing on financial markets is necessary for determining how the government is affecting the availability of funds for other borrowers. One measure of federal borrowing—debt held by the public—provides a straightforward assessment of that borrowing and captures most of the impact on the availability of funds for other borrowers; it is roughly equivalent to the sum of all previous annual budget deficits minus surpluses (see Chapter 1). All else being equal, an increase in the government's borrowing reduces the funds available for others, putting upward pressure on interest rates and reducing private investment.

Another measure—debt held by the public net of financial assets—is a more complicated measure; it reflects the fact that when the government lends money or acquires financial assets, such as debt and equity securities issued by private firms, those funds flow into investment activities. Therefore, that measure subtracts from debt held by the public the value of assets the government has acquired through its various lending activities and through efforts to address the recent financial crisis. Debt held by the public net of financial assets provides a more comprehensive picture of the government's financial condition and its overall impact on credit markets than does debt held by the public. Calculating that measure is not straightforward, however, because neither the universe of such assets nor the method for valuing them is well defined.

Another important purpose for which measures of debt are helpful is to assess the government's overall financial condition, taking into account not only debt that the government has already incurred (and the assets it has purchased) but also commitments the government has made for the future. Debt held by the public, with or without an adjustment for the government's financial assets, does not account for future obligations. Assessing the government's future financial status requires additional information. Measures that have been used for that purpose include gross federal debt and debt subject to limit; however, two other measures—projected changes in debt held by the public as a share of gross domestic product and the fiscal gap—provide a clearer picture of the government's future obligations.

Gross debt equals federal debt held by the public plus Treasury securities held by federal trust funds and other government accounts. That measure is not a good indicator of the government's future obligations because the value of Treasury securities held by trust funds and other government accounts measures only some of the commitments the government has made for the future, and it includes some amounts that may not represent future commitments at all. Moreover, those securities represent internal transactions of the government and thus have no direct effect on credit markets.

Debt subject to limit is the amount of gross federal debt subject to the ceiling on the issuance of debt established by law. It differs in only small ways from gross federal debt. It too includes internal transactions of the government that have no direct effect on credit markets and is not a meaningful measure of the government's future commitments.

Measures that explicitly account for the government's future fiscal condition are better indicators of that condition than are either gross debt or debt subject to limit. One useful barometer is projections of changes in debt held by the public relative to gross domestic product; such projections indicate whether the government's participation in credit markets is expected to grow faster or slower than economic output. Another useful gauge is the fiscal gap, which measures the immediate change in spending or revenues that would be necessary to make the projected debt-to-GDP ratio the same at the end of a given period as at the beginning of the period. The fiscal gap quantifies the projected long-term shortfall of revenues relative to outlays in present-value terms—that is, as a single number that describes a set of future flows in terms of an equivalent lump sum received or spent today. Those two measures are not addressed in this report but are used extensively in other Congressional Budget Office publications.[18]

Debt Held by the Public Net of Financial Assets

Until a few years ago, financial assets held by the government were relatively small and largely composed of the Treasury's cash balances, loans made by various federal credit programs, and private equities owned by the National Railroad Retirement Investment Trust. During the past five years, however, the volume of direct loans made to students—which represent an asset to the government in the form of future payments of principal and interest—has more than doubled, and it is projected to expand greatly in the next decade. In addition, the government's holdings of financial assets grew substantially during the recent financial crisis.

The assets the government has acquired affect its financial position, and the effect can be viewed in several ways. If those assets are sold, the proceeds can be used to pay down a portion of the federal debt. If, instead, the government retains those assets, they will generate inflows from interest, dividends, and repayments of principal that will reduce the government's future need to borrow.

Because federal asset holdings have increased relative to debt held by the public, debt held by the public net of financial assets has taken on increased importance as a measure of the government's financial position. In total, at the end of 2010, the government held financial assets with an estimated value of more than $1 trillion.[19] Subtracting that amount from the $9.0 trillion in debt held by the public results in debt held by the public net of financial assets of about $8.0 trillion. Debt held by the public is currently equal to about 62 percent of GDP, and debt net of financial assets amounts to about 55 percent of GDP. A difference of 5 to 8 percentage points between the two measures persists through 2020 in CBO's most recent baseline projections (see Table 2-1).

Cash

One of the largest financial assets that the Treasury currently holds is cash. The Treasury's cash flows fluctuate during the year according to the timing of tax collections and spending; as a result, the Treasury maintains deposits of varying amounts at the Federal Reserve and in banks throughout the country. Between 2000 and 2007, the Treasury ended the fiscal year with an average balance of about $50 billion. However, balances have been much higher over the past three years because, since September 2008, the Treasury has deposited additional funds with the Federal Reserve to help it conduct monetary policy and stabilize the financial system. The balance for the Treasury's deposits through that program—known as the Supplementary Financing Program—reached a high of more than $550 billion in November 2008. As of the end of 2010, the SFP had a balance of $200 billion and the Treasury's total operating cash balance was $310 billion. CBO expects that the SFP will be eliminated by the end of 2011.

Credit Programs

The value of loans, guarantees, and asset purchases of federal credit programs at the end of 2010 totaled $712 billion. That amount represents the present value of the expected future cash flows from those assets and obligations. For loan guarantees—such as those made by the Federal Housing Administration—the present value is based on expected income from fees to be received net of payouts to cover losses from defaults. The value of direct loans and asset purchases totaled $745 billion at the end of 2010; that amount was partially offset by net liabilities of $32 billion from guaranteed loan programs.

Most of the government's direct loans are made by the Department of Education to students pursuing postsecondary education. At the end of 2010, based on data reported by the Department of the Treasury, the estimated value of student loans outstanding was $341 billion. CBO projects that, with the recent expansion of that program in the Health Care and Education Reconciliation Act of 2010 (P.L. 111-152), those assets will grow to nearly $1.4 trillion by the end of 2020.

To help promote stability in the mortgage market and lessen upward pressure on mortgage rates, from September 2008 to December 2009 the Treasury purchased mortgage-backed securities issued by Fannie Mae and

Table 2-1. CBO's Projections of Debt Held by the Public Net of Financial Assets, 2010 to 2020

	Actual 2010	2011	2012	2013	2014	2015	2016	2017	2018	2019	2020
				In Billions of Dollars							
Debt Held by the Public	9,018	9,958	10,742	11,373	11,902	12,495	13,165	13,837	14,497	15,232	16,024
Financial Assets (Net of liabilities)											
Treasury's operating cash balance	310	40	40	40	40	40	40	40	40	40	40
Credit programs											
Department of Education programs	341	453	564	670	769	868	964	1,060	1,159	1,263	1,374
Mortgage-backed securities	173	164	156	148	141	134	127	121	115	109	103
Troubled Asset Relief Program	122	97	82	67	52	37	22	7	0	0	0
Other	77	95	118	134	144	153	156	160	168	177	185
Subtotal, credit programs	712	809	921	1,019	1,106	1,192	1,269	1,347	1,442	1,549	1,663
National Railroad Retirement Investment Trust	21	19	18	17	15	14	13	12	10	9	8
Othera	-29	-29	-29	-29 -	-29	-29	-29	-29	-29	-29	-29
Total	1,014	840	950	1,046	1,132	1,217	1,293	1,370	1,463	1,569	1,681
Debt Held by the Public Net of Financial Assets	8,003	9,119	9,793	10,327	10,770	11,279	11,873	12,467	13,034	13,663	14,343
				As a Percentage of Gross Domestic Product							
Debt Held by the Public	62.2	65.7	68.1	68.1	67.0	67.1	67.5	67.8	68.1	68.6	69.2
Debt Held by the Public Net of Financial Assets	55.2	60.2	62.1	61.8	60.6	60.5	60.9	61.1	61.2	61.5	61.9

Sources: Congressional Budget Office; Department of the Treasury.

a. Includes other cash and monetary assets (mostly related to transactions with the International Monetary Fund) offset by liabilities such as interest accrued but not yet paid to the public.

Freddie Mac in the open market. Those securities, which have various maturity dates, generate payments of interest and principal. CBO assumes that the Treasury will hold those securities until they mature. Overall, the Treasury purchased more than $200 billion in such securities; the present value of the remaining holdings was $173 billion at the end of 2010.

As part of its activities related to the recent financial crisis, the Treasury also acquired numerous assets through the Troubled Asset Relief Program. Such assets were valued by the Treasury (using a present-value calculation that includes an adjustment for market risk) at $122 billion at the end of 2010. The assets were obtained through three kinds of transactions:

- Capital purchases and other support for financial institutions;
- Financial assistance to automakers and related businesses; and
- Investment partnerships designed to increase liquidity in the securitizetion markets.

The three largest sets of assets outstanding are preferred stock and warrants obtained in the Capital Purchase Program, securities of the American International Group, and securities of the automotive industry.[20] The Treasury expects that a large share of those assets will eventually be repurchased by the issuers or sold to other market participants.

The outstanding value of assets related to other credit activities is projected to increase from $77 billion in 2010 to $185 billion in 2020. Those totals include other direct loan programs (such as those for rural areas and small businesses) and guaranteed loan programs (such as those for housing).

Gross Federal Debt

In addition to selling securities to the public, the Treasury issues securities to various accounts of the federal government. Gross federal debt consists of the debt held by the public plus debt issued to such government accounts.

Trust funds hold about 90 percent of the debt issued to government accounts. Although trust funds are designated as such by law, there is no substantive difference between them and other types of funds. Those other types include special funds (such as the fund the Department of Defense uses to finance its health care program for military retirees), revolving funds (such as the Federal Employees' Group Life Insurance fund), and public enterprise funds (such as the Postal Service fund). All of the major trust funds in the budget and many other government funds invest in special, nonmarketable Treasury securities known as the government account series.

At the end of 2010, gross federal debt totaled $13.5 trillion—about $9.0 trillion in debt held by the public and $4.5 trillion in debt held by government accounts. CBO projects that, under current law, gross federal debt will increase in every year of the 2011–2020 period, reaching $23.1 trillion in 2020 (see Table 2-2). That increase stems primarily from the projected growth in debt held by the public, which is projected to exceed $15.2 trillion by the end of that year.

The largest balances among the government accounts are in the two Social Security trust funds—the Old-Age and Survivors Insurance and Disability Insurance trust funds. By the end of 2010, those trust funds had accrued close to $2.6 trillion; in CBO's projections, that combined balance rises to $3.8 trillion by the end of 2020 (see Table 2-3). In addition, the retirement funds for federal civilian and military employees held a combined $1.1 trillion in government account securities at the end of 2010; those balances will increase to slightly more than $2 trillion over the next 10 years, CBO projects. By the end of 2020, the total balance of all trust funds will climb to more than $6 trillion, and the total held by all government accounts will reach $7 trillion.

Because the trust funds are part of the federal government, transactions between them and the Treasury are intragovernmental and have no net effect on federal borrowing from the public or on the total budget. Different sorts of transactions occur: Any surplus cash flow during the year from the activities of a program with a trust fund is retained by the Treasury, and the trust fund is credited with a corresponding amount of nonmarketable Treasury securities. The Treasury then uses the cash to finance the government's ongoing activities. When a trust fund's expenses exceed its cash income, the agency administering the trust fund redeems its Treasury securities for cash as needed; the Treasury must obtain that cash from tax revenues or other sources of income or by borrowing from the public. In addition, most securities in the government account series earn interest at rates similar to those on publicly issued debt, and the Treasury issues additional debt to the trust funds in the amount of the interest payments. However, the issuance of the securities, the payments of interest, and any other transactions between the Treasury and the trust funds have no net effect on the budget.

Federal trust funds, then, are essentially an accounting mechanism. The balances in the trust funds (in the form of government securities) are assets to the individual programs (such as Social Security) but liabilities to the rest of the government.

Table 2-2. CBO's Projections of Federal Debt, 2010 to 2020

(Billions of dollars)	Actual 2010	2011	2012	2013	2014	2015	2016	2017	2018	2019	2020
Debt Held by the Public at the Beginning of the Fiscal Year	7,545	9,018	9,958	10,742	11,373	11,902	12,495	13,165	13,837	14,497	15,232
Changes to Debt Held by the Public											
Deficit	1,294	1,066	665	525	438	507	585	579	562	634	685
Other means of financing	179	-126	118	107	90	86	86	93	99	101	107
Debt Held by the Public at the End of the Fiscal Year	9,018	9,958	10,742	11,373	11,902	12,495	13,165	13,837	14,497	15,232	16,024
Debt Held by Government Accounts	4,509	4,638	4,803	5,002	5,236	5,510	5,796	6,095	6,413	6,740	7,062
Gross Federal Debt	3,527	14,596	15,545	16,376	17,138	18,005	18,961	19,932	20,911	21,972	23,086
Debt Subject to Limita	13,511	14,581	15,530	16,361	17,123	17,992	18,948	19,919	20,898	21,960	23,073
Memorandum:											
Debt Held by the Public as a											
Percentage of Gross Domestic Product	62.2	65.7	68.1	68.1	67.0	67.1	67.5	67.8	68.1	68.6	69.2

Source: Congressional Budget Office.

a. Differs from gross federal debt primarily because most debt issued by agencies other than the Treasury and the Federal Financing Bank is excluded from the debt limit. The current limit is $14,294 billion.

The resources to redeem government securities in the trust funds and thereby pay for benefits or other spending in some future year must be generated from taxes, income from other government sources, or borrowing from the public in that year. Trust funds have an important legal meaning in that their balances are a measure of the amounts that the government has the legal authority to spend for certain purposes under current law, but they have little relevance in an economic or budgetary sense.

More than 200 trust funds exist in the federal budget, but the bulk of holdings of government securities is concentrated in just a few funds. Most of the difference between gross federal debt and debt held by the public is that the former includes balances held by the Social Security trust funds. Those balances reflect a decision by policymakers to set the payroll tax dedicated to Social Security over the past few decades such that the program's revenues would be greater than the program's outlays in anticipation of rising benefit costs as the baby-boom generation retires. The debt held by those trust funds measures the amount by which Social Security revenues have exceeded outlays in the past, but it does not measure the program's future financial burden. Even with the securities held by the trust funds and with a dedicated future stream of revenues, by 2039 those resources will be insufficient to pay the full benefits that will accrue under current law, CBO projects. At the same time, the balances in the Social Security trust funds have significant legal implications: By law, total Social Security benefits cannot exceed amounts available in the trust funds, and the benefits projected to be paid will be smaller in 2039 and beyond than the benefits specified in law.[21]

Beyond Social Security, the amount of government debt held by trust funds and other government accounts bears even less of a relationship to the government's future financial burdens: For example, the Medicare program holds little government debt relative to its expected future costs.

Debt Subject to Limit

The Congress has traditionally placed a limit on the amount of debt the Treasury can issue. Before World War I, the Congress generally had to approve each separate debt issue. Since the passage of the Second Liberty Bond Act in 1917, the limit has gradually evolved into an overall dollar ceiling on debt.

Table 2-3. CBO's Projections of Trust Fund Balances, 2010 to 2020

	Actual 2010	2011	2012	2013	2014	2015	2016	2017	2018	2019	2020
Social Security	2,586	2,675	2,675	2,787	2,916	3,055	3,200	3,344	3,490	3,629	3,757
Civilian Retirementa	797	816	835	855	876	897	920	944	970	997	1,026
Military Retirement	282	330	382	439	501	569	644	725	813	909	1,012
Medicare	350	314	294	278	269	268	264	265	273	278	279
Unemployment Insurance	19	24	27	29	31	41	50	61	75	95	114
Highway and Airport	37	30	18	7	-3	-13	-22	-30	-37	-45	-52
Otherb	86	87	88	90	91	93	96	99	102	105	108
Total	4,157	4,276	4,320	4,485	4,680	4,912	5,152	5,408	5,685	5,968	6,244
Memorandum:											
Railroad Retirement (Non-Treasury holdings)c	21	20	19	18	17	16	15	13	12	11	9

Source: Congressional Budget Office.

a. Includes the Civil Service Retirement and Disability Fund and the Employees and Retired Employees Health Benefits Fund.

b. Primarily the federal employees' life insurance fund, Superfund, and various insurance trust funds for veterans.

c. The Railroad Retirement and Survivors' Improvement Act of 2001 established an entity, the National Railroad Retirement Investment Trust, that is allowed to invest in securities not issued by the Treasury, such as stocks and corporate bonds. The trust holds a small amount of Treasury securities, included in the "Other" category.

The modern concept of debt subject to limit was created in 1941, when the Congress placed a limit on the total amount of federal debt that could be outstanding at any given time. Since then, the Congress has passed numerous increases to the debt limit—commonly known as the "debt ceiling"— some of which have been temporary and many of which have been permanent.

What the Debt Limit Covers

Debt subject to limit includes virtually all of gross federal debt. It excludes debt issued by other federal agencies that the Treasury does not control and that generally lack the full faith and credit of the U.S. government (such as securities issued by the Tennessee Valley Authority).

It also excludes debt issued by Fannie Mae, Freddie Mac, and the Federal Financing Bank (FFB)—an arm of the Treasury created in 1973 and authorized to issue up to $15 billion of its own debt. (Debt issued by Fannie Mae and Freddie Mac is also not included in other standard measures of federal debt; see Box 1-1 in Chapter 1).

Options for the Treasury When Debt Approaches the Limit

CBO estimates that the debt ceiling, which was raised to $14.294 trillion in February 2010, will be reached in the next several months. At that point, barring Congressional action to raise the ceiling, the Treasury would have to stop issuing additional debt for a period of time and, instead, use alternative strategies for managing its cash and debt to continue to fund government activities. Because the government will be running a significant deficit in 2011, such strategies will allow the government to continue operating for only a limited time without further borrowing.

Suspending Sales of Nonmarketable Securities

One of the first actions the Treasury has often taken when the debt limit was about to be reached has been to suspend the sale of securities in the state and local government series.[22] That action does not immediately clear any room under the debt ceiling and has virtually no impact on the markets for public debt because securities in the state and local government series are not sold or traded in secondary markets. However, suspending sales of those securities removes some uncertainty about the future path of debt because the timing and amounts of issuances to state and local governments is difficult to predict.

Trimming or Delaying Auctions of Marketable Securities

In the weeks leading up to a point at which the debt would reach the limit, the Treasury may pare back auction amounts for marketable securities or postpone one or more auctions. Although the delay of a small number of auctions in the past has not led to significant increases in the cost of borrowing, continuous delays could adversely affect the willingness of credit markets to absorb the issuance of debt.

Suspending Issuance of Maturing Cash Management Bills in the Supplementary Financing Program

The Treasury currently has $200 billion outstanding in cash management bills allocated to the SFP. If total borrowing approached the debt limit, the Treasury could decide not to refinance those bills when they mature. That option would give the Treasury up to an additional $200 billion in borrowing room.

Suspending Flows and Redeeming Securities in Government Accounts

When the debt limit is close to being reached, the Treasury has the option to delay the addition of deposits to certain accounts and to redeem securities in three funds: the Thrift Savings Plan's G Fund, the Civil Service Retirement and Disability Fund (CSRDF), and the Exchange Stabilization Fund (ESF).[23] Because the G Fund is invested in 1-day securities, the Secretary of the Treasury is able, at any time, to disinvest up to the full balance of the fund (that is, to withdraw or reduce the balance); that balance was $124 billion at the end of 2010. The CSRDF has special rules regarding balances and how they can be disinvested; the amount that can be redeemed early cannot exceed the amount of benefit payments expected during the period until a new debt ceiling is enacted. The Treasury also can suspend investment of all additional receipts to the fund if they will cause a breach of the debt limit. The ESF currently holds $20 billion in Treasury securities, which the Treasury can decide not to reinvest when they mature. After the debt limit has been raised, the Treasury must restore any losses of interest (as well as principal) to the G Fund and CSRDF but has no such obligation to the ESF.

Swapping Debt with the Federal Financing Bank

Debt issued by the FFB, which cannot exceed $15 billion, is not subject to the debt limit.[24] The Treasury can swap securities that are counted toward the debt limit for securities issued by the FFB, thus decreasing the debt subject to limit, and has used that option in the past. About $10 billion in outstanding FFB securities are currently held by the CSRDF; issuing an additional $5 billion in FFB securities to that fund in exchange for Treasury securities would currently give the Treasury about $5 billion of additional room for borrowing from the public.

Consequences of Having a Limit on Debt

By itself, setting a limit on the debt is an ineffective means of controlling deficits because the decisions that necessitate borrowing are made through other legislative actions. By the time an increase in the debt ceiling comes up for approval, it is too late to avoid paying the government's pending bills without incurring serious negative consequences. However, because increases in the debt limit have been essential, the process of considering such increases tends to bring debt levels to the forefront of policy debate.

INTEREST PAYMENTS AND RECEIPTS

The government pays and collects interest in various ways; its net interest outlays are equal to interest paid minus interest received. Net interest outlays are dominated by the interest paid to holders of the debt that the Department of the Treasury issues to the public. The Treasury also issues debt to trust funds and other federal government accounts, but the payment of interest to those accounts is an intragovernmental transaction that has no effect on net interest and no effect on the budget deficit. Other federal accounts also pay and receive interest for a variety of reasons.

Historical and Projected Net Interest Outlays

The federal government's net interest payments depend primarily on interest rates and the amount of debt held by the public. Other factors, such as the rate of inflation and the maturity structure of outstanding securities, also affect interest costs (for example, long-term bonds generally carry higher interest rates than do short-term bills). Interest rates are determined by a combination of market forces and the policies of the Federal Reserve. Debt held by the public is mostly determined by cumulative budget deficits, which reflect policy choices about spending and revenues, economic conditions, and other factors. The maturity structure of the debt is determined by the borrowing policy implemented by the Treasury, which issues a variety of short- and long-term debt securities (as described in Chapter 1).

Historical Trends in Net Interest Outlays

Net interest outlays as a percentage of gross domestic product have fluctuated over the past 40 years, from a low of 1.3 percent to a high of 3.3 percent (see Figure 3-1). Through most of the 1970s, net interest totaled no more than 1.5 percent of GDP. At the end of that decade, however, the growing amount of debt relative to the size of the economy and higher real (inflation-adjusted) interest rates began to boost interest costs; by 1985, net interest outlays as a percentage of GDP were twice as large as they had been in the mid-1970s. For the following decade, net interest payments remained at about 3 percent of GDP, but narrower budget deficits (and then surpluses) and lower interest rates for many securities pushed that figure down in the late 1990s. Net interest outlays continued to decline as a percentage of GDP in the early 2000s, returning to a level similar to that in the early 1970s.

Although debt held by the public has surged in the past few years to its highest level relative to GDP since the early 1950s, net interest outlays have remained low relative to GDP because interest rates on Treasury securities have fallen to remarkably low levels (see Figure 3-2). Rates on 3-month Treasury bills plummeted from an average of almost 5 percent in 2007 to an average of just over 0.1 percent in 2010. Similarly, rates on 10-year Treasury notes and 30-year bonds have dropped from an average of close to 5 percent in 2007 to an average of about 3 percent and 4 percent, respectively, in 2010. As a result, despite the dramatic increase in debt held by the public—from 36 percent of GDP at the end of 2007 to 62 percent at the end of 2010—net interest outlays as a percentage of GDP fell from 1.7 percent in 2007 to 1.3 percent in 2009 and rose only marginally, to 1.4 percent, in 2010.

CBO's Baseline Projections

Under the Congressional Budget Office's August 2010 baseline budget projections, which reflect the assumption that current laws and policies affecting the budget will remain unchanged, growing debt and rising interest rates are projected to substantially boost the cost of interest on the government's debt.[25] In those projections, debt held by the public increases to almost 70 percent in 2020. Moreover, interest rates climb from their current levels to levels similar to those in the late 1990s. The rate on 3-month Treasury bills is forecast to increase from an average of about 0.2 percent in 2010 to 5.0 percent in 2016 and then to stay at that rate through 2020. The rate on 10-year Treasury notes is projected to rise from an average of 3.4 percent in 2010 to 5.9 percent in 2016 and to remain there through the end of the decade.

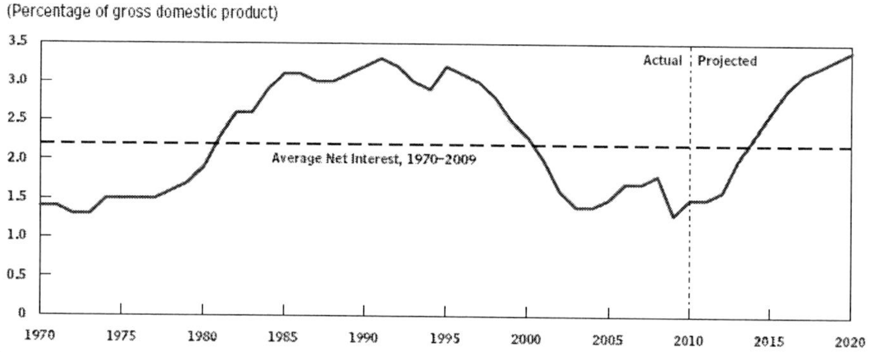

Source: Congressional Budget Office; historical data are based on information from the Office of Management and Budget.

Figure 3-1. Net Interest, 1970 to 2020.

Given those projections, spending on net interest would rise from $197 billion in 2010 to $778 billion in 2020 (see Table 3-1). Relative to GDP, net interest outlays would increase to 3.4 percent in 2020, more than double the percentage in 2010 and the highest percentage since 1991 (see Figure 3-1).

Alternative Scenarios

Future interest rates and deficits are uncertain and will be affected by legislative actions, economic developments, and other factors. To illustrate how changes in those variables would affect interest costs, CBO has estimated those costs under different assumptions regarding interest rates and future deficits.[26]

Higher Interest Rates

Interest rates on government securities that were higher than CBO projects would raise interest outlays on new borrowing and on debt that must be refinanced. If interest rates for all newly issued Treasury securities were 1 percentage point higher in each year than the rates in the August baseline, net interest payments would be higher in each year of the projection period, CBO estimates, by amounts rising from $13 billion in 2011 to $185 billion in 2020. From 2011 through 2020, interest costs would be higher by more than $1 trillion (see Table 3-2). (Lower interest rates would have the opposite effect.)

That increase in interest payments would stem from two sources: the cost of applying higher rates to the debt projected in the baseline (the direct effect) and the interest paid on the additional sums borrowed to pay those higher rates. The $13 billion in additional outlays in 2011 would stem mostly from the direct effect on rates. Of that amount, more than $8 billion would be attributable to short-term securities and $4 billion to medium- and long-term securities (including savings bonds and state and local government securities).[27]

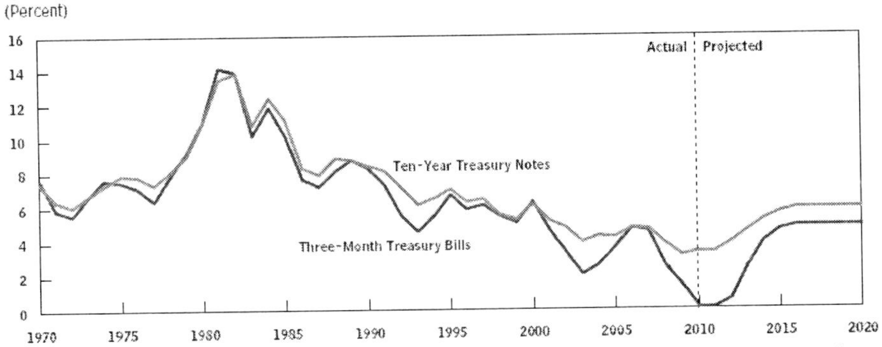

Source: Congressional Budget Office; historical data are based on information from the Federal Reserve.

Figure 3-2. Interest Rates on Three-Month Treasury Bills and Ten-Year Treasury Notes, 1970 to 2020.

In later years, the effect of a change in rates would become much more pronounced for medium- and long-term securities. Added interest for those securities would amount to $605 billion over the period, compared with $220 billion for short-term securities. The larger deficits generated by the higher interest payments would require the Treasury to borrow additional funds. That extra borrowing would result in further increases in the annual cost of servicing the debt, which would grow to $50 billion in 2020 and would total $185 billion over the 10-year period.

Additional Borrowing

If budget deficits were higher than CBO projects, net interest payments also would be higher. (Lower deficits would have the opposite effect.) To illustrate the effect of higher deficits (and therefore higher debt) on interest costs, CBO estimated the impact of two different increases in the government's borrowing.

First, CBO examined a $100 billion increase in borrowing in 2011. That borrowing also would boost interest outlays in the same year by $1 billion, excluding any potential effects on interest rates. The effect of that additional borrowing would increase interest outlays by a cumulative total of $43 billion from 2011 through 2020. (Costs in later years would stem from the compounding effect of increasing the debt in 2011.)

Second, the agency calculated the effect on interest payments of borrowing that was $100 billion greater in each year of the projection period (excluding additional interest costs). That borrowing would lead to additional interest outlays of $272 billion over the 10-year period, if interest rates were not affected.

Gross Interest on Treasury Debt Securities

In 2010, interest paid by the Treasury on all of its debt issuances totaled $413 billion (see Table 3-1). Nearly half of that total represents payments to other entities (such as trust funds) within the federal government; the remainder is paid to owners of Treasury debt issued to the public. CBO projects that, under current law, gross interest will exceed $1.1 trillion by 2020; the majority of that growth stems from increased interest paid on debt held by the public, which is projected to almost quadruple under current law during the coming decade.

Interest Received by Trust Funds

Federal trust funds and other government accounts hold about $4.5 trillion in Treasury securities; more than 90 percent of that total is held by trust funds. Similar in composition to debt held by the public, the securities held by trust funds and other government accounts consist of bills, notes, bonds, inflation-protected securities, and zero-coupon bonds. However, the interest paid on those securities has no net budgetary impact because it is credited to accounts elsewhere in the budget.

In 2010, trust funds were credited with $186 billion of such intragovernmental interest, CBO estimates, mostly for the Social Security trust funds and the Civil Service Retirement and Disability Fund (see Table 3-1). Over the 2011–2020 projection period, CBO estimates, the trust funds' interest receipts will total about $2 trillion.

Other Interest

Although federal net interest outlays are dominated by interest on the Treasury's borrowing from the public, the government also pays and receives interest from other transactions. The federal budget includes about 50 accounts that reflect those interest payments and collections. Collections of interest are shown in the budget as negative outlays—that is, as offsets to spending. Some of those 50 accounts have no net effect on the budget because they are intragovernmental and reflect payments or receipts from other federal budget accounts.

Overall, the government receives more interest in the category of "other interest" than it pays out, primarily because of interest received from nonbudgetary financing accounts, which track the cash flows of credit programs. Net receipts to accounts in that category have risen from more than $7 billion in 2006 to $15 billion in 2009 and to more than $28 billion in 2010 (see Table 3-3). CBO projects that those receipts will continue to climb, surpassing $100 billion by 2019. Most of the projected increase stems from larger payments of interest from credit financing accounts, particularly payments from the financing accounts for the federal student loan program.

Table 3-1. CBO's Baseline Projections of Federal Interest Outlays, 2010 to 2020 (Billions of dollars)

	Actual 2010	2011	2012	2013	2014	2015	2016	2017	2018	2019	2020	Total	
												2011-2015	2011-2020
Gross Interest on Treasury Debt Securities[a]	413	438	463	543	637	739	835	915	995	1,070	1,149	2,820	7,783
Interest Received by Trust Funds													
Social Security	-119	-116	-114	-116	-122	-130	-140	-152	-163	-175	-186	-598	-1,415
Other trust funds[b]	-67	-67	-55	-59	-52	-54	-55	-55	-61	-65	-70	-287	-593
Subtotal	-186	-183	-169	-174	-174	-184	-195	-206	-224	-240	-256	-884	-2,007
Other Interest[c]	-28	-30	-35	-42	-52	-63	-74	-85	-95	-104	-114	-221	-693
Other Investment Income[d]	-2	*	*	*	-1	-1	-1	-1	-1	*	*	-2	-5
Total, Net Interest	197	225	259	326	410	492	564	623	676	726	778	1,712	5,079

Source: Congressional Budget Office.

Note: * = between -$500 million and zero.

a. Gross interest is the total interest paid by the Treasury; it does not include interest costs on debt issued by agencies other than the Treasury (primarily the Tennessee Valley Authority).

b. Mainly the Civil Service Retirement, Military Retirement, Medicare, and Unemployment Insurance trust funds.

c. Primarily interest from the financing accounts for federal credit programs.

d. Earnings on private investments by the National Railroad Retirement Investment Trust.

Table 3-2. Alternative Scenarios for Net Interest Outlays, 2011 to 2020 (Billions of dollars)

	2011	2012	2013	2014	2015	2016	2017	2018	2019	2020	Total, 2011-2020
August 2010 Baseline (Net interest)	225	259	326	410	492	564	623	676	726	778	5,079
				Effect of Higher Interest Rates							
Direct Effect of an Increase of 1 Percentage											
Point in Interest Ratesa											
Short-term securities	8	17	18	19	21	23	25	27	30	33	220
Medium- and long-term securitiesb	4	23	40	52	61	71	79	86	91	98	605
Treasury inflation-protected securities	*	1	1	2	2	3	3	3	4	4	24
Subtotal	12	40	59	73	84	96	107	116	125	135	849
Debt Servicec	*	1	2	6	11	17	24	32	40	50	184
Total	13	41	62	79	95	113	131	149	165	185	1,033
				Effect of Additional Borrowing							
One-Time Increase in Borrowing											
of $100 Billion in 2011	1	2	2	4	4	5	6	6	7	7	43
Annual Increase in Borrowing of $100 Billion	1	3	7	13	21	29	37	45	54	63	272

Source: Congressional Budget Office.

Note: * = between zero and $500 million.

a. Costs on the amount of new borrowing and refinancing of maturing securities.

b. Includes savings bonds and securities issued to state and local governments.

c. Additional borrowing needed to cover additional interest costs.

Interest Paid to and Collected from the Credit Financing Accounts

Under the Federal Credit Reform Act of 1990, the budget shows the subsidy costs of the government's direct loans and loan guarantees rather than the cash flows associated with those activities. The subsidy is the discounted present value of all future cash flows: generally, disbursements and repayments net of default losses in the case of direct loans; and fees, payments for defaults, and recoveries in the case of loan guarantees.

To track those cash flows and reconcile them with subsidy costs that are recorded in the budget, the Treasury created credit financing accounts (see Chapter 1). Although the cash flows for those accounts are not included in the budget totals, they influence the Treasury's borrowing requirements.

How the Accounts Work

For a direct loan made by the government, a financing account receives a subsidy payment from the budget account for that loan program (recorded in the budget as an outlay) and borrows from the Treasury the rest of the funds needed to make the loan. Some or all of that borrowing by the financing account is repaid to the Treasury over time as the direct loan made by the government is repaid. Meanwhile, the financing account pays interest to the Treasury on any outstanding balance. Those interest receipts are recorded in the budget as negative outlays.

Therefore, direct loans result in three interest flows:

- Borrowers pay interest on their loans, which is credited to the financing account;
- The financing account, in turn, pays interest to the Treasury on the money it borrowed to make the loans; and
- The Treasury pays interest on the public debt that it issued to provide the necessary resources for the financing account.

Loan guarantees operate differently from direct loans. With a guarantee, the government agrees to repay, in the event of default, loans made by nongovernmental institutions. Financing accounts for guaranteed loan programs usually receive cash inflows when a loan is made; the inflows often include guarantee fees from lenders and subsidy payments from the budget account for that guarantee program. Any defaults on loans that would require a payment from the account typically occur later. As a result, a financing account for a guarantee program generally runs a surplus with the Treasury, which credits the financing account with interest on that sum, generating positive outlays in the budget.

Table 3-3. Other Interest, 2006 to 2010
(Billions of dollars)

	2006	2007	2008	2009	2010
Interest Paid to and Collected from Credit Financing Accounts	-5.4	-5.0	-5.7	-13.4	-22.8
Interest Receipts					
Interest earned on deposits in tax and loan accounts	-0.9	-1.2	-0.6	*	*
Interest from unemployment loans to states	*	*	*	0	0
Other	-0.8	-1.0	-0.8	-0.5	-0.4
Interest Expenses					
Interest paid on tax refunds	4.2	3.3	4.5	2.4	2.2
Interest paid to Resolution Funding Corporation	2.0	2.0	1.4	2.1	2.3
Other	0.2	*	*	*	*
Intragovernmental Interest					
Interest from the Federal Financing Bank	-0.4	-0.7	-0.8	-0.6	-1.0
Earnings on MERHCF investments	-3.8	-4.0	-7.8	-1.1	-5.1
Earnings on USPS Retiree Health Care Fund	0	*	-1.2	-1.4	-1.5
Interest from the Nuclear Waste Fund	-0.5	-0.8	*	-1.1	-1.2
Other	-1.8	-2.6	-1.8	-1.4	-0.9
Total	-7.3	-10.1	-12.9	-15.0	-28.5

Source: Congressional Budget Office based on data from the Office of Management and Budget.

Notes: Negative numbers represent the government's interest income; positive numbers represent its interest expenses.

* = between -$500 million and $500 million.

MERCHF = Medicare-Eligible Retiree Health Care Fund; USPS = U.S. Postal Service.

Amounts of Interest Received from the Financing Accounts

In 2010, the interest transactions between the Treasury and the financing accounts yielded net receipts to the Treasury of almost $23 billion, up from about $13 billion in 2009. (Interest flows between the Treasury and credit financing accounts, like other intragovernmental transfers, have no effect on borrowing by the Treasury.) The student loan program currently represents the bulk of the balances in financing accounts and, therefore, the largest volume of interest flowing to the Treasury (a net receipt to the Treasury of $11 billion for 2010).

The flows of interest payments to the Treasury related to direct student loans will steadily increase in coming years because the Health Care and Education Reconciliation Act of 2010 (Public Law 111-152) terminated the Federal Family Education Loan program, which guaranteed loans to student borrowers made through private lenders such as banks, credit unions, and some postsecondary institutions. As new activity occurs entirely through direct loans rather than guaranteed loans, the additional borrowing that the financing account requires to fund the additional loans will result in higher interest payments from that account to the Treasury.

Two other financing accounts that make sizable interest payments to the Treasury are those for the Troubled Asset Relief Program and for the Treasury's purchase of mortgage-backed securities. Both programs were created in the fall of 2008 in response to the financial crisis, and in each case the budget recorded only the estimated subsidy provided to the program. To carry out their missions, however, both programs required funding that was not directly recorded in the budget. The TARP was established to purchase or insure troubled assets to promote stability in financial markets. Funding from the Treasury was used to purchase preferred stock from financial institutions; to provide assistance to American International Group, General Motors, and Chrysler; and for a number of other purposes.[28] The MBS purchase program sought to increase liquidity in the secondary mortgage market by increasing the demand for those securities. In terms of the federal budget, both programs operate like direct loan programs: The Treasury provided funds to their respective financing accounts for disbursement, and the financing accounts now pay interest to the Treasury on that borrowing. The budget recorded net receipts of $10 billion in interest from the financing accounts for the TARP and MBS purchases in 2010.

Other credit financing accounts include those for the Rural Utilities Service, for several housing programs under the Department of Housing and Urban Development, and for many other, smaller credit programs.

Other Interest Receipts

Most other accounts in the category of "other interest" record inflows to the government from interest payments or earnings on investments; such collections are recorded as negative outlays in the budget. Historically, the largest collection accounts have been those that record interest earnings on deposits in so-called tax and loan accounts at banks. Interest on loans to states' unemployment funds are another source of such receipts.

Interest Earned on Deposits in Tax and Loan Accounts

The federal government, like individuals and businesses, maintains a working balance of cash to cover current expenditures. Because the timing and amount of receipts never precisely match disbursements, the amount of funds at the Treasury's disposal varies widely over short periods, especially around quarterly tax dates and payment dates for Social Security, Medicare, and veterans' benefits.

The Treasury generally holds its cash balances in two types of accounts—demand deposits (similar to noninterest-bearing checking accounts) at Federal Reserve Banks and tax and loan accounts at commercial banks located throughout the country. Those commercial banks qualify as special depositories to maintain tax and loan accounts for the Treasury; businesses can use the accounts to deposit taxes withheld from employees' paychecks, corporate income taxes, and other recurring payments. In exchange for the short-term use of those funds, the participating banks pay interest to the Treasury at the greater of zero and the federal funds rate minus one-quarter of one percentage point.[29]

Balances in the tax and loan accounts are highly volatile. During 2010, overall daily closing balances ranged from a low of $62 million to a high of roughly $3 billion and averaged just under $2 billion. Interest received from the tax and loan accounts has declined significantly in the past two years: The total interest received in 2010 was close to zero, down from about $40 million in 2009 and about $600 million in 2008—the result of a significantly lower federal funds rate (which declined from 2.9 percent in 2008 to 0.3 percent in 2009 and to 0.2 percent in 2010) and the Treasury's decision in 2008 to limit the balances being held in the tax and loan depositories to $2 billion.

Interest from Unemployment Loans to States

When states have insufficient funds in their Unemployment Trust Fund accounts, they may receive advances from the federal government to pay unemployment benefits. States pay no interest on those advances if they repay them within a fiscal year, but after that they generally are charged interest. However, provisions of the American Recovery and Reinvestment Act (P.L. 111-5) made borrowing interest-free through December 2010. As of October 2010, balances on the unemployment loans to states exceeded $40 billion, and CBO projects that interest payments on such balances will total $1 billion to $2 billion per year beginning in 2011 if interest forgiveness is not extended beyond 2010.

Other Interest Expenses

A few accounts in the category of "other interest" track interest payments to individuals or organizations outside the federal budget. The largest of such accounts include interest payments on certain tax refunds and the interest paid on bonds sold in the 1980s and 1990s to help resolve the savings and loan crisis.

Interest Paid on Tax Refunds

The Treasury pays interest on individual, corporate, and excise tax refunds that are paid more than 45 days after the filing date. Interest on such refunds is generally dominated by interest on income tax returns that have been amended or audited. Corporate and individual taxpayers can file an amended return for a previous year; if a refund is due, the Internal Revenue Service calculates interest from the initial filing date. Over the 2011–2020 period, CBO estimates, such payments will total between $2 billion and $4 billion a year.

Interest Paid to the Resolution Funding Corporation

REFCORP is a government-sponsored enterprise created in 1989 to provide initial funding for the Resolution Trust Corporation (RTC). REFCORP issued $31.2 billion in bonds to finance the RTC's efforts to resolve the savings and loan crisis in the late 1980s and early 1990s. The interest owed on those obligations totals $2.6 billion annually and is paid quarterly by several entities. The Federal Home Loan Banks (FHLBanks) are currently required by statute to contribute 20 percent of their annual net earnings (about $500 million to $700 million per year) toward REFCORP's interest payment. The Treasury pays the remainder of the interest due, roughly $2.1 billion annually, or about 80 percent of the total. The Federal Deposit Insurance Corporation has also made periodic contributions to REFCORP's interest payments, but the amount and frequency of such payments are not statutorily mandated.

CBO currently projects that the FHLBanks will complete their required interest payments on REFCORP bonds in 2011 and, as a result, that the Treasury will begin to make the full annual interest payment of $2.6 billion in 2012. The REFCORP bonds begin to mature in 2019, and all will have matured by April 2030, at which point interest payments will cease.

Intragovernmental Interest

Some accounts in the "other interest" category have no net effect on the budget because they are intragovernmental and reflect receipts from other federal budget accounts. Such accounts include the Federal Financing Bank (FFB), the retiree health care funds for certain members of the military and employees of the U.S. Postal Service (USPS), the Nuclear Waste Fund, and some other federal entities.

Interest from the Federal Financing Bank

The FFB is an arm of the Treasury Department that acts as a financial intermediary for a few federal agencies, government corporations, and government-sponsored enterprises; it was created in 1973 to reduce federal borrowing costs and improve debt management by assisting with borrowing by those entities. The FFB borrows directly from the Treasury and charges the agencies its own cost of borrowing plus one-eighth of one percentage point. Payments of interest from the FFB to the Treasury have been less than $1 billion annually in recent years but are projected to increase (to as much as $6 billion) because of higher loan activity (particularly by the Department of Energy's Advanced Technology Vehicles Manufacturing program and the Rural Utilities Service). Those interest payments have no net effect on the budget; they appear as outlays in the FFB's budget account and as offsetting receipts in "other interest." As of September 30, 2010, the FFB portfolio totaled $60 billion.

Medicare-Eligible Retiree Health Care Fund

MERCHF was established by the National Defense Authorization Act for 2001 and began operation in 2003. The fund pays for the health care costs of retirees of the uniformed services and their dependents and survivors, once those individuals are eligible for Medicare. The Treasury makes payments into the fund to cover future benefits and also pays interest on the balance in the fund. Those balances are therefore increasing rapidly. In 2009, payments to the fund (excluding interest) totaled $21.3 billion, and outlays to cover health care expenses totaled $8.4 billion. Through 2020, CBO projects, payments to the fund will continue to be significantly higher than outlays. In 2020, those payments into the fund (other than interest) will be about $34 billion, compared with $16 billion in outlays. As a result, the interest credited to the fund will also grow dramatically, from $5 billion in 2010 to almost $22 billion by 2020, CBO projects.

U.S. Postal Service Retiree Health Benefits Fund

This fund was established in 2006 as a way of financing the health benefits of USPS retirees beginning in 2017. (The costs of health benefits for USPS retirees are currently paid from the annual operating funds of the Postal Service.) The USPS is required to make annual payments of between $5 billion and $6 billion to the fund through 2016, and those payments are used to purchase Treasury securities. As of September 30, 2010, the fund had a balance of nearly $42 billion, and its interest earnings in 2010 totaled $1.5 billion. CBO projects that interest earnings over the 2011–2020 period will total about $42 billion.

Nuclear Waste Fund

This fund pays for activities related to the permanent disposal of high-level nuclear waste from commercial and defense-related sources. The income it receives from fees paid by commercial producers of nuclear power is invested in long-term Treasury securities. The fund's portfolio consists primarily of zero-coupon Treasury bonds; the interest credited to the fund totaled about $1 billion in 2010 and, CBO projects, will average about $2 billion per year over the 2011–2020 period.

Other Intragovernmental Interest Receipts

The Congress allows certain government corporations and federal entities to borrow from the Treasury to finance part of the costs of their programs. That borrowing authority is conferred through either permanent authorizing language or annual appropriations. The Treasury and the individual agencies decide on the terms of the loan, depending on the needs of the program being financed. The agencies' borrowing includes long- and short-term debt, and interest rates vary by program.

Both the payment and the receipt of those intragovernmental interest transactions are accounted for in the federal budget, but because those amounts are offsetting, they do not affect the budget deficit. In particular, the interest payment is booked as an outlay for the participating agency, and the receipt of that payment is recorded as an offsetting receipt in the Treasury's intragovernmental interest account. Interest on loans to the Bonneville Power Administration, the National Flood Insurance Fund, and the Helium Fund accounted for nearly two-thirds of the other $915 million in intragovernmental interest paid to the Treasury in 2010.

Other Investment Income

The National Railroad Retirement Investment Trust (NRRIT), a tax-exempt entity that is independent of the federal government, is charged with managing and investing the assets of the Railroad Retirement program. However, because the functions of the NRRIT are considered to be federal in nature, the earnings and losses of the program are accounted for in the budget in the general category of net interest.

The NRRIT is authorized to invest the assets of the Railroad Retirement fund in a diversified investment portfolio, like the portfolios of private-sector retirement plans. About 95 percent of the current portfolio is invested in private holdings that are actively managed by the NRRIT; the remaining 5 percent is invested in nonmarketable Treasury securities. The trust's average earnings for 2004 through 2007 totaled about $3 billion a year, but market declines in recent years have produced losses from the NRRIT's investments. In 2008 and 2009, the trust had losses of $6 billion and $350 million, respectively. At the end of 2009, the balance in the Railroad Retirement fund was about $23 billion, down from a high of nearly $33 billion in 2007. To project the NRRIT's future earnings, CBO assumes a rate of return equal to the average projected rate on new Treasury issues; under that assumption, CBO projects that earnings will average about $500 million per year through 2020 (see Table 3-1 on page 28).

APPENDIX: PUBLIC DEBT OUTSTANDING AT THE END OF THE FISCAL YEAR

The Department of the Treasury issues two broad types of securities to the public: marketable and non-marketable. Marketable securities—bills, notes, bonds, and Treasury inflation-protected securities—are auctioned at regular intervals during the year and can be resold. Nonmarketable securities, such as savings bonds, are not sold at auction and cannot be resold. Tables A-1 and A-2 show the outstanding value of each type of debt at the end of fiscal years 1990 through 2010.

Table A-1. Marketable Public Debt Outstanding at the End of the Fiscal Year, 1990 to 2010

Fiscal Year	Bills[a]		Notes		Bonds		Treasury Inflation-Protected Securities[b]		Total (Billions of dollars)
	Billions of Dollars	Percentage of Total	Billions of Dollars	Percentage of Total	Billions of Dollars	Percentage of Total	Billions of Dollars	Percentage of Total	
1990	482	23	1,218	59	377	18	n.a.	n.a.	2,078
1991	565	24	1,388	58	423	18	n.a.	n.a.	2,376
1992	634	24	1,566	59	462	17	n.a.	n.a.	2,647
1993	658	23	1,734	60	497	17	n.a.	n.a.	2,840
1994	697	23	1,868	61	512	17	n.a.	n.a.	3,077
1995	742	23	1,980	61	523	16	n.a.	n.a.	3,245
1996	761	22	2,099	62	543	16	n.a.	n.a.	3,403
1997	702	20	2,122	62	576	17	24	1	3,425
1998	638	19	2,009	61	610	18	59	2	3,316
1999	653	20	1,829	57	644	20	92	3	3,218
2000	616	21	1,611	54	635	21	115	4	2,978
2001	735	25	1,433	49	613	21	135	5	2,915
2002	868	28	1,522	49	593	19	139	4	3,121
2003	918	27	1,799	52	577	17	166	5	3,460
2004	961	25	2,109	55	552	14	223	6	3,846
2005	910	22	2,328	57	521	13	307	8	4,066
2006	908	21	2,445	57	534	12	396	9	4,284
2007	955	22	2,456	55	561	13	457	10	4,428
2008	1,484	28	2,623	50	579	11	524	10	5,210
2009	1,986	28	3,773	54	677	10	551	8	6,988
2010	1,784	21	5,253	62	846	10	594	7	8,476

Source: Congressional Budget Office based on data from the Department of the Treasury.

Note: n.a. = not applicable.

a. Reported at face value. b. Inflation-adjusted amount.

Table A-2. Nonmarketable Public Debt Outstanding at the End of the Fiscal Year, 1990 to 2010 (Billions of dollars)

Fiscal	Savings	State and Local	Thrift	Zero-Coupon Bonds[a]			
Year	Bonds	Government Series	Savings Plan	Foreign	Domestic	Other[b]	Total
1990	122	161	7	4	2	3	299
1991	134	158	9	5	3	3	311
1992	148	158	12	4	4	*	326
1993	167	149	15	6	3	1	341
1994	176	137	18	6	3	1	342
1995	181	113	21	7	4	1	327
1996	184	96	23	6	4	3	316
1997	183	112	25	6	4	1	331
1998	181	164	26	8	5	1	386
1999	180	168	29	6	5	1	390
2000	178	153	32	5	5	1	374
2001	186	146	37	4	6	6	386
2002	193	144	45	3	6	7	398
2003	202	148	51	4	7	22	434
2004	204	158	56	3	7	7	436
2005	204	225	64	3	8	10	513

Fiscal	Savings	State and Local	Thrift	Zero-Coupon Bonds[a]			
Year	Bonds	Government Series	Savings Plan	Foreign	Domestic	Other[b]	Total
2006	204	239	72	2	8	10	535
2007	197	297	81	2	9	12	598
2008	194	260	101	2	10	10	578
2009	192	216	113	2	11	7	542
2010	189	193	124	2	11	7	526

Source: Congressional Budget Office based on data from the Department of the Treasury.

Note: * = between zero and $500 million.

a. CBO's estimate of current economic value.

b. Includes mostly claims funds and asset forfeiture funds (starting in 2001), foreign series bills, tax and loss bonds issued by the Mortgage Guaranty Insurance Corporation, U.S. notes and silver certificates, and, in 2003, depository compensation securities

.

End Notes

[1] Debt held by the public consists mostly of securities that the Department of the Treasury issues to raise cash to fund the activities of the government, including the securities sold to pay off maturing securities; it also includes a small amount of securities issued by other agencies, mainly the Tennessee Valley Authority.

[2] See, for example, Congressional Budget Office, *The Long-Term Budget Outlook* (June 2010, revised August 2010).

[3] The inflation adjustment to principal is based on the non-seasonally adjusted consumer price index for all urban consumers (CPI-U). The adjustment to the value of outstanding TIPS is made on a daily basis but is not paid until maturity. For more information, see Treasury Direct, "TIPS: Rates and Terms," www.treasurydirect.gov/indiv/research/indepth/tips/res_tips_rates.htm.

[4] In a reopening, the Treasury issues an additional amount of a previously issued security. The reopened security has the same maturity date and interest rate as the original security but has a different issue date and, usually, a different purchase price.

[5] Zero-coupon bonds do not provide coupon payments over the life of the security. Instead, they are sold at a discount to face value, and the full face value is paid at maturity.

[6] For additional details on savings bonds, see Treasury Direct, "Products in Depth," http://treasurydirect.gov/indiv/research/ indepth/indepth.htm.

[7] Demand deposits may be withdrawn at any time without advance notice.

[8] Present value is defined as a single number that expresses a flow of current and future income (or payments) in terms of an equivalent lump sum received (or paid) today.

[9] In this study, the term "credit programs" generally refers to direct loans and loan guarantees and to some purchases of financial assets (such as the acquisition of preferred stock by the TARP).

[10] Mortgage-backed securities are issued by financial institutions to investors. The payments of interest and principal on the MBSs are backed by the payments on a package of mortgages.

[11] The Dodd-Frank Wall Street Reform Act of 2010 (P.L. 111-203) reduced the Treasury's authority under the TARP to $475 billion. For more information on the TARP, see Congressional Budget Office, *Report on the Troubled Asset Relief Program—November 2010* (November 2010).

[12] For more information, see Federal Reserve Bank of New York, "Statement Regarding Supplementary Financing Program," www.ny.frb.org/markets/statement_091708.html.

[13] Fannie Mae and Freddie Mac, both of which are in federal conservatorship, also are permitted to issue debt independently of the Treasury.

[14] Unlike most other costs in the budget, interest costs are recorded as outlays when they accrue, not when they are paid.

[15] For information on other duties of the Federal Reserve, see Box 1 in Congressional Budget Office, *The Budgetary Impact and Subsidy Costs of the Federal Reserve's Actions During the Financial Crisis* (May 2010). That study also discusses the other methods the Federal Reserve has used to conduct monetary policy during the recent financial crisis and severe recession.

[16] For more information on general government debt net of financial liabilities, see Organisation for Economic Co-operation and Development, "EO Sources—Notes to statistical annex tables 25–33: Fiscal balances and public indebtedness," Annex Table 33, www.oecd.org/document/25/0,3343,en_2649_34109_ 33702745_1_1_1_1,00.html.

[17] U.S. debt held by the public was 53 percent of GDP at the end of fiscal year 2009. Using the OECD's measure of debt—general government debt net of financial liabilities—that share was 60 percent at the end of calendar year 2009.

[18] See, for example, Congressional Budget Office, *The Long-Term Budget Outlook* (June 2010, revised August 2010).

[19] That total does not include assets held by the Federal Reserve. Because of its need for flexibility and independence in setting monetary policy, the Federal Reserve is not part of the executive branch but is considered an independent entity within the government; its receipts and expenditures are not included directly in the federal budget, although it remits its excess earnings to the Treasury.

[20] For more information on the TARP, see Chapter 1 of this report and Congressional Budget Office, *Report on the Troubled Asset Relief Program—November 2010* (November 2010).

[21] See Congressional Budget Office, *Social Security Policy Options* (July 2010).

[22] For more information on state and local government securities, see Chapter 1.

[23] The TSP is a retirement program for federal employees similar to a private-sector 401(k) plan; the G Fund is one component of the TSP and is solely invested in Treasury securities. The CSRDF is the trust fund for federal employees' retirement plans. The ESF is a fund controlled by the Treasury for the purpose of stabilizing exchange rates.

[24] For more information on the Federal Financing Bank, see Chapter 3.

[25] See Congressional Budget Office, *The Budget and Economic Outlook: An Update* (August 2010).

[26] The alternative scenarios do not take into account any changes in GDP, inflation, or other economic factors; as a result, revenues and noninterest outlays are unchanged. The interest-rate scenario also does not reflect the effect of higher interest rates on interest-sensitive programs, such as student loans.

[27] Changes in interest rates have the greatest impact on shorter-term securities in the first year because those securities will be refinanced much more often in that year than will medium- and long-term securities. Within a given year, all bills outstanding will have to be refinanced at least once.

[28] For more information on the TARP, see Congressional Budget Office, *Report on the Troubled Asset Relief Program—November 2010* (November 2010).

[29] The federal funds rate is the interest rate that financial institutions charge each other for overnight loans of their monetary reserves.

In: Federal Debt, Interest Costs… ISBN: 978-1-61324-288-9
Editors: A. V. Martinez, K. M. Schulz

Chapter 2

THE DEBT LIMIT: HISTORY AND RECENT INCREASES*

D. Andrew Austin and Mindy R. Levit

SUMMARY

Total debt of the federal government can increase in two ways. First, debt increases when the government sells debt to the public to finance budget deficits and acquire the financial resources needed to meet its obligations. This increases *debt held by the public*. Second, debt increases when the federal government issues debt to certain government accounts, such as the Social Security, Medicare, and Transportation trust funds, in exchange for their reported surpluses. This increases *debt held by government accounts*. The sum of *debt held by the public* and *debt held by government accounts* is the total federal debt. Surpluses reduce debt held by the public, while deficits raise it. Total federal debt outstanding was $14,025 billion on December 31, 2010. The U.S. Treasury projects the federal debt will reach its statutory limit in spring 2011, although tax policy, spending changes, and economic trends, will affect that timing. Without a debt limit increase, funding federal operations after the middle of 2011 may be complicated.

---

* This is an edited, reformatted and augmented version of a Congressional Research Services publication, dated January 6, 2011.

A statutory limit has restricted total federal debt since 1917 when Congress passed the Second Liberty Bond Act. Congress has voted to raise the debt limit ten times since 2001. Deficits each year since 2001 and the persistent increases in debt held by government accounts repeatedly raised the debt to or near the limit in place at the time. Congress raised the limit in June 2002, and by December 2002 the U.S. Department of the Treasury asked Congress for another increase, which was passed in May 2003. In June 2004, the Treasury asked for another debt limit increase. After Congress recessed in mid-October 2004 without acting, the Secretary of the Treasury told Congress that the actions he was taking to avoid exceeding the debt limit would suffice only through mid-November. Congress approved a debt limit increase in a post-election session, which the President signed on November 19, 2004. In 2005, reconciliation instructions in the FY2006 budget resolution (H.Con.Res. 95) included a debt limit increase. With no action having been taken by December 2005, the Secretary of the Treasury sent several letters warning Congress that the Treasury would exhaust its options to avoid default by mid-March 2006. Congress passed an increase in mid-March, which the President signed on March 20. The House indirectly approved legislation (H.J.Res. 43) to raise the debt limit by $850 billion to $9,815 billion. The Senate approved the resolution on September 27, 2007, and it was signed by the President two days later.

The current economic slowdown led to sharply higher deficits in recent years, which led to a series of debt limit increases. The Housing and Economic Recovery Act of 2008 (H.R. 3221), signed into law (P.L. 110-289) on July 30, 2008, included a debt limit increase. The Emergency Economic Stabilization Act of 2008 (H.R. 1424), signed into law on October 3 (P.L. 110-343), raised the debt limit again. The debt limit rose a third time in less than a year to $12,104 billion with the passage of American Recovery and Reinvestment Act of 2009 on February 13, 2009 (ARRA; H.R. 1), which was signed into law on February 17, 2009 (P.L. 111-5).

The House's adoption of the conference report on the FY2010 budget resolution (S.Con.Res. 13) on April 29, 2009, triggered the automatic passage of H.J.Res. 45 to raise the debt limit to $13,029 billion. In August 2009, Treasury reportedly said that the debt limit would be reached in mid-October, although it later stated that the limit would not be reached until December 2009. H.R. 4314, passed by the House on December 16, 2009, and by the Senate on December 24, raised the debt limit to $12,394 billion when the President signed the measure (P.L. 111-123) on December 28. On January 28, the Senate passed an amended version of H.J.Res. 45, which the House passed on February 4 and the President signed on February 12 (P.L. 111-139), raising the limit to $14,294 billion. This report, written with the assistance of Joseph McCormack, will be updated as events warrant.

INTRODUCTION

The statutory debt limit applies to almost all federal debt.[1] The limit applies to federal debt held by the public (that is, debt held outside the federal government itself) and to federal debt held by the government's own accounts. Federal trust funds, such as Social Security, Medicare, Transportation, and Civil Service Retirement accounts, hold most of this internally held debt.[2] The government's surpluses or deficits determine essentially all of the change in debt held by the public.[3] The government's on-budget fiscal balance, which excludes a small U.S. Postal Service net surplus or deficit and a large Social Security surplus of payroll taxes net of paid benefits, does not directly affect debt held in government accounts.[4] Increases or decreases in debt held by government accounts result from net financial flows into accounts holding the debt, such as the Social Security Trust Fund. Legal requirements and government accounting practices also affect levels of debt held by government accounts.[5]

On December 31, 2010, total federal debt outstanding was $14,025 billion, and debt subject to the debt limit was $13,973 billion, about $320 billion below the current statutory debt limit of $14,294 billion.[6] In August 2010, the Congressional Budget Office estimated that the FY2011 budget deficit will total $1,066 billion, which suggests that federal debt will reach its limit some time in spring 2011, unless spending or revenue policies are altered or the debt limit is again raised.[7] Some Wall Street analysts expect federal debt to near its limit in April or May 2011, although many factors, including federal tax policy and strength of the economic recovery, could affect federal debt trends.[8] On January 6, 2011, Treasury Secretary Geithner sent a letter to Senate Majority Leader Harry Reid stating that federal debt limit would likely reach its statutory limit between March 31 and May 16, 2011.[9] Without a debt limit increase, the U.S. Treasury may face difficulty in funding federal operations after the middle of 2011.

The Debt Limit and the Treasury

Standard methods of financing federal activities or meeting government obligations used by the U.S. Department of Treasury (Treasury) can be hobbled when federal debt nears its legal limit. The government's income and outlays vary over the course of the year, producing monthly surpluses and deficits that affect the level of debt, whether or not the government has a surplus or deficit for the entire year. The government accounts holding federal debt also can experience monthly deficits and surpluses, even for the major accounts that usually show annual surpluses. The ability to borrow is a central to Treasury cash management systems that handle fluctuations in federal revenues and outlays. When federal debt has neared the debt limit in the past, limiting the U.S. Treasury's borrowing authority, financial management has become more complicated.

If the U.S. Treasury were precluded from borrowing due to a binding debt limit in times when federal outlays outpaced revenues, the government would no longer meet all of its legal obligations in a timely manner.[10] If the limit prevents the Treasury from issuing new debt to manage short-term cash flows or to finance an annual deficit, the government may be unable to obtain the cash needed to pay its bills or it may be unable to invest the surpluses of designated government accounts (federal trust funds) in federal debt as generally required by law. In either case, the Treasury is left in a bind; the law requires that the government's legal obligations be paid, but the debt limit may prevent it from issuing the debt that would allow it to do so on time.

Among other consequences, a sustained inability to pay obligations on time could hinder the U.S. Treasury's ability to borrow on advantageous terms in the future. A delay in interest payments on Treasury securities would trigger a default, which would risk causing serious negative repercussions for economies and financial markets around the world. Default might be avoided in such situations by delaying other types of federal payments and transfers. A government that delays payment of an obligation, in effect, borrows from vendors, contractors, beneficiaries, state and local governments, or employees who are not paid on time. In some cases, delaying payments incurs interest penalties under some statutes such as the Prompt Payment Act, which directs the government to pay interest penalties to contractors if it does not pay them by the required payment date,[11] and the Internal Revenue Code, which requires the government to pay interest penalties if tax refunds are delayed beyond a certain date.[12]

Past Treasury Secretaries, when faced with a nearly binding debt ceiling, have used special strategies to handle cash and debt management responsibilities. Actions taken in the past include suspending sales of nonmarketable debt, postponing or downsizing marketable debt auctions, and withholding receipts that would be transferred to certain government trust funds. Congress has authorized the Treasury Secretary to invoke a "debt issuance suspension period" to use some of these strategies using the Civil

Service Retirement Fund and the Thrift Savings Fund, along with the authority to make those funds whole after an easing of the debt constraint.[13]

Some U.S. Treasury responses to the credit crunch that began in mid 2007 created balance sheet items that might expand options available to the Treasury Secretary. The U.S. Treasury, however, is unlikely to maintain smooth debt management operations indefinitely in the face of a continuing imbalance between federal revenues and outlays without an increase in the debt limit.

Why Have a Debt Limit?

The debt limit can hinder the Treasury's ability to manage the federal government's finances, as noted above. In extreme cases, when the federal debt is very near its statutory limit, the Treasury must take unusual and extraordinary measures to meet federal obligations.[14] While the debt limit has never caused the federal government to default on its obligations, it has at times caused great inconvenience and has added uncertainty to Treasury operations.

The debt limit also provides Congress with the strings to control the federal purse, allowing Congress to assert its constitutional prerogatives to control spending.[15] The debt limit also imposes a form of fiscal accountability that compels Congress and the President to take visible action to allow further federal borrowing when the federal government spends more than it collects in revenues. In the words of one author, the debt limit "expresses a national devotion to the idea of thrift and to economical management of the fiscal affairs of the government."[16] On the other hand, some budget experts have advocated elimination of the debt limit, arguing that other controls provided by the modern congressional budget process established in 1974 have superseded the debt limit, and that the limit does little to alter spending and revenue policies that determine the size of the federal deficit.[17]

A Brief History of the Federal Debt Limit

Origins of the Federal Debt Limit

The statutory limit on federal debt began with the Second Liberty Bond Act of 1917,[18] which helped finance the United States' entry into World War

I.[19] By allowing the Treasury to issue long-term Liberty Bonds, which were marketed to the public at large, the federal government held down its interest costs.[20]

Before World War I, Congress often authorized specific loans, such as the Panama Canal loan, or allowed the Treasury to issue specific types of debt instruments, such as certificates of indebtedness, bills, notes and bonds.[21] In other cases, especially in time of war, Congress provided the Treasury with discretion, subject to broad limits, to choose debt instruments.[22] For example, the 1898 War Revenue Act (30 Stat. 448-470) that funded Spanish-American War costs granted the Treasury Secretary the authority to issue $100 million in certificates of indebtedness with maturities under a year and $400 million in longer term notes and bonds.[23] Proponents of the Act made clear their intention to allow the Treasury Secretary substantial administrative leeway.[24]

With the passage of the Second Liberty Bond Act, Congress enacted aggregate constraints on certificates of indebtedness and on bonds that allowed the Treasury greater ability to respond to changing conditions and more flexibility in financial management. Debt limit legislation in the following two decades also set separate limits for different categories of debt, such as bills, certificates, and bonds.

In 1939, Congress eliminated separate limits on bonds and on other types of debt, which created the first aggregate limit that covered nearly all public debt.[25] This measure gave the Treasury freer rein to manage the federal debt as it saw fit. Thus, the Treasury could issue debt instruments with maturities that would reduce interest costs and minimize financial risks stemming from future interest rate changes.[26] On the other hand, although the Treasury was delegated greater independence of action, the debt limit on the eve of World War II was much closer to total federal debt than it had been at the end of World War I. For example, the 1919 Victory Liberty Bond Act (P.L. 65-328) raised the maximum allowable federal debt to $43 billion, far above the $25.5 billion in total federal debt at the end of FY1919.[27] By contrast, the debt limit in 1939 was $45 billion, only about 10% above the $40.4 billion total federal debt of that time.

World War II and After

The debt ceiling was raised to accommodate accumulating costs for World War II in each year from 1941 through 1945, when it was set at $300 billion.[28] After World War II ended, the debt limit was reduced to $275 billion. Because the Korean War was mostly financed by higher taxes rather than by increased debt, the limit remained at $275 billion until 1954. After 1954, the debt limit was reduced twice and increased seven times, until March 1962 when it again reached $300 billion, its level at the end of World War II. Since March 1962, Congress has enacted 74 separate measures that have altered the limit on federal debt.[29] Most of these changes in the debt limit were, measured in percentage terms, small in comparison to changes adopted in wartime or during the Great Depression. Some recent increases in the debt limit, however, were large in dollar terms. For instance, in May 2003, the debt limit increased by $984 billion.

THE DEBT CEILING IN THE LAST DECADE

During the four years (FY1998-FY2001) the government ran surpluses, federal debt held by intergovernmental accounts grew by $855 billion and debt held by the public fell by almost $450 billion. Since FY2001, however, debt held by the public has grown due to persistent and substantial budget deficits. Debt held in government accounts also has grown, in large part because Social Security payroll taxes have exceeded payments of beneficiaries. **Table 1** shows components of debt in current dollars and as percentages of gross domestic product (GDP).[30]

Figure 1 shows the components of federal debt as shares of gross domestic product (GDP) from FY1940 through FY2010.[31] Federal debt held by government accounts has grown steadily since 1980. Debt held by the public, which changes in response to total surpluses or deficits, grew as a share of GDP through the mid-1990s. After FY1992, deficits shrank, and from FY1998 through FY2001 the federal government ran surpluses.[32] Those surpluses, along with rapid GDP growth, reduced debt held by the public as a percentage of GDP. When large deficits returned and GDP growth slowed in the early 2000s, debt held by the public as a share of GDP again increased.

Smaller deficits in FY2006 and FY2007 led to smaller increases in publicly held debt. The total FY2007 deficit fell to 1.2% of GDP according to CBO.[33] Financial turmoil in 2007 and 2008 and a subsequent recession that began in late 2007 led to federal actions taken to stabilize the housing and financial markets. The recession reduced federal revenues and increased federal spending, leading to large deficits and a series of debt limit increases.

Table 1. Components of Debt Subject to Limit, FY1996-FY2010
(in billions of current dollars and as percentage of GDP)

		Debt Subject to Limit					
End of Fiscal Year	Debt Limit	Total		Held by Government Accounts		Held by the Public	
		$ Billion	% of GDP	$ Billion	% of GDP	$ Billion	% of GDP
1996	$5,500	$5,137.2	65.7%	1,432.4	18.3%	3,704.8	47.4%
1997	5,950	5,327.6	64.2	1,581.9	19.0	3,745.8	45.1
1998	5,950	5,439.4	62.2	1,742.1	19.9	3,697.4	42.3
1999	5,950	5,567.7	60.1	1,958.2	21.1	3,609.5	38.9
2000	5,950	5,591.6	57.0	2,203.9	22.4	3,387.7	34.5
2001	5,950	5,732.8	56.6	2,436.5	24.1	3,296.3	32.5
2002	6,400	6,161.4	58.9	2,644.2	25.3	3,517.2	33.6
2003	7,384	6,737.6	61.4	2,846.7	25.9	3,890.8	35.5
2004	7,384	7,333.4	62.5	3,056.6	26.0	4,276.8	36.4
2005	8,184	7,871.0	64.0	3,301.0	26.9	4,570.1	37.2
2006	8,965	8,420.3	64.2	3,610.4	27.5	4,809.8	36.7
2007	9,815a	8,921.3	65.4	3,903.7	28.6	5,017.6	36.8
2008	10,615b	9,960.0	70.0	4,180.0	29.4	5,780.3	40.6
2009	12,104c	11,909.8	84.1	4,358.0	30.8	7,551.9	53.3

		Debt Subject to Limit					
		Total		Held by Government Accounts		Held by the Public	
End of Fiscal Year	Debt Limit	$ Billion	% of GDP	$ Billion	% of GDP	$ Billion	% of GDP
2010	14,294d	13,510.8	92.1	4,585.7	31.3	9,022.8	61.5
Change during FY1998 - FY2001		$405.2		$854.6		$-449.5	
Change during FY2002 - FY2010		$7,778.0		$2,073.1		$5,704.9	

Source: U.S. Department of the Treasury, Financial Management Service, *Treasury Bulletin*, June 2001 and December 2006. Bureau of the Public Debt, *Monthly Statement of Public Debt*, various issues. CRS calculations.

Notes: For the fiscal years 1996 through 2000, the amounts held by government accounts and held by the public are approximations. In 2001, the Treasury publications began distinguishing holders of debt subject to limit. The numbers in the table showing this breakdown for FY1996 through FY2000 were calculated by subtracting debts of the Federal Financing Bank, an arm of the Treasury whose debt is not subject to limit, from total debt held by government accounts. This calculation approximates the amount of that debt subject to limit. This approximation overestimates debt by billions of dollars because estimates of unamortized discount are unavailable. This adjusted amount was then subtracted from total debt subject to limit to produce an approximate measure of debt held by the public subject to limit. Because the amount held by government accounts is overestimated, the resulting measure of debt held by the public subject to limit is underestimated. Totals may not sum due to rounding.

a Debt limit increased September 29, 2007, to $9,815 billion.

b The debt limit was increased twice in 2008—to $10,615 billion on July 30 and then to $11,315 billion on October 3, at the start of FY2009.

c Debt limit was increased February 17, 2009, to $12,104 billion.

d. Debt limit was increased February 12, 2010, to $14,294 billion.

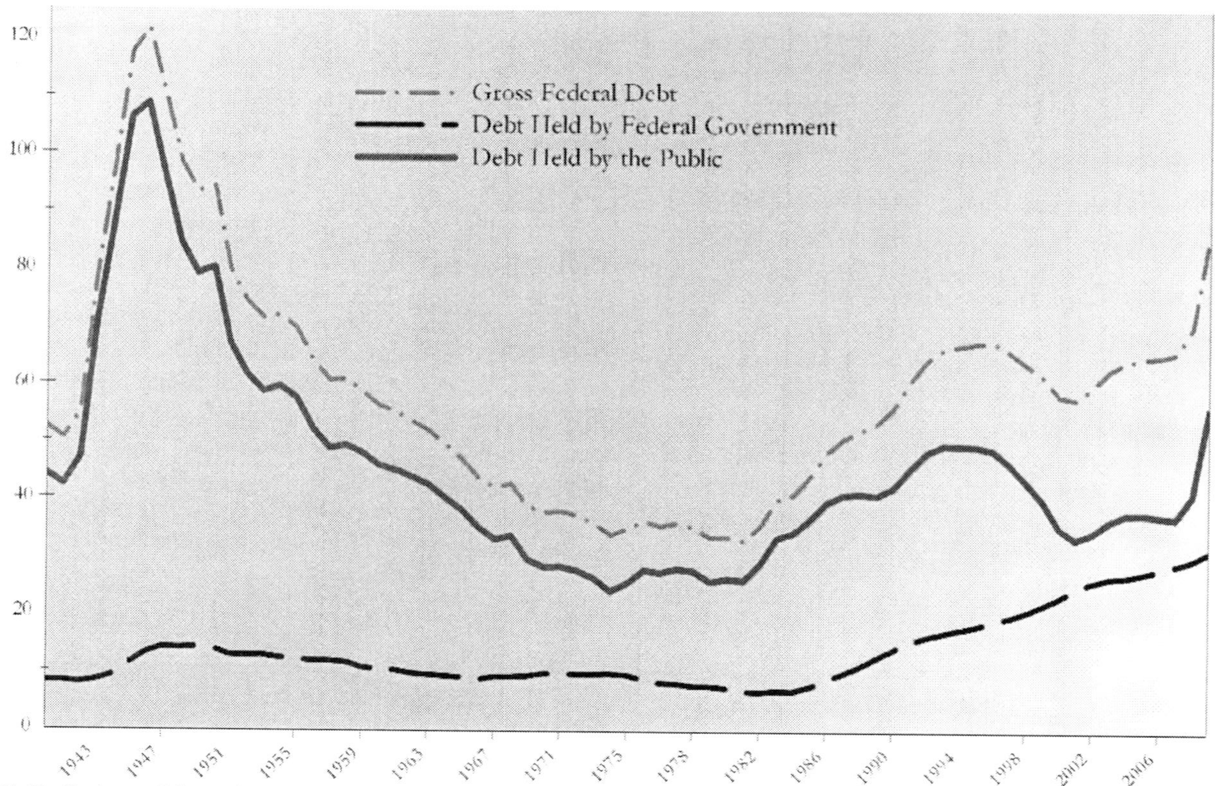

Source: OMB, Budget of the United States for FY2010, Historical Tables, February 2009; Mid-Session Review, August 2009.

Figure 1. Components of Federal Debt As a Percentage of GDP, FY1940-FY2009.

The Debt Limit Issue in 2002

Accumulating debt in government accounts produced most of the pressure on the debt limit that occurred early in 2002. As deficits reemerged in FY2002, increases in debt held by the public added to the pressure on the debt limit in the spring of 2002. During the four fiscal years with surpluses (FY1998-FY2001), the increases in federally held debt and decreases in debt held by the public produced a net increase of $405 billion in total debt subject to limit. At the beginning of FY2002 (October 1, 2001), debt subject to limit was within $217 billion of the existing $5,950 billion debt limit.[34] Between then and the end of May 2002, debt subject to limit increased by another $217 billion, divided between a $117 billion increase in debt held by government accounts and a $100 billion increase in debt held by the public, putting the debt close to the $5,950 billion limit. **Table A-1**, presented in the **Appendix**, shows month-by-month debt totals and accumulations from September 2001 through December 2010.

In the fall of 2001, the Administration recognized that a deteriorating budget outlook and continued growth in debt held by government accounts were likely to lead to the debt limit soon being reached. In early December 2001, it asked Congress to raise the debt limit by $750 billion to $6,700 billion. As the debt moved closer to and reached the debt limit over the first six months of FY2002, the Administration asked Congress repeatedly to increase the debt limit, warning of adverse financial consequences were the limit not raised.

On April 4, 2002, the Treasury held debt below the limit by invoking its legislatively mandated authority to suspend reinvestment of government securities in the G-Fund of the federal employees' Thrift Savings Plan (TSP). This allowed the Treasury to issue new debt and meet the government's obligations. On April 15, debt subject to limit stood at $5,949,975 million, just $25 million below the limit. Once April 15 tax revenues flowed in, the Treasury "made whole" the G-Fund by restoring all of the debt that had not been issued to the TSP over this period and crediting the fund with interest it would have earned on that debt.[35] By the end of April, debt subject to limit had fallen back $35 billion below the limit.

Resolving the Debt Limit Issue in 2002

By the middle of May 2002, debt subject to limit had again risen to within $15 million of the statutory limit. At the FY2002 average spending rate, $15 million equaled about five minutes of federal outlays. The Treasury, for the second time in 2002, used its statutory authority to avoid a default. The Treasury's financing problems, however, would persist without an increase in the debt limit. On May 14, the Treasury asked Congress to raise the debt limit or enact other statutory changes allowing the Treasury to issue new debt. A Treasury news release stated "absent extraordinary actions, the government will exceed the statutory debt ceiling no later than May 16," and that

> a "debt issuance suspension period" will begin no later than May 16 [2002].... [This] allows the Treasury to suspend or redeem investments in two trust funds, which will provide flexibility to fund the operations of the government during this period.[36]

The Treasury reduced federal debt held by these government accounts by replacing it with noninterest-bearing, non-debt instruments, which enabled it to issue new debt to meet the government's obligations. The Treasury claimed these extraordinary actions would suffice, at the latest, through June 28, 2002. Without a debt limit increase by that date, the Treasury indicated it would need to take other actions to avoid breaching the ceiling. By June 21, the Treasury had postponed a regular securities auction, but took no other actions. With large payments and other obligations due at the end of June and at the beginning of July, the Treasury stated it would soon exhaust all options to issue debt and fulfill government obligations, putting the government on the verge of a default.

During May and June 2002, Congress took steps to increase the debt limit. The FY2002 supplemental appropriations bill (H.R. 4775) passed by the House on May 24 included, after extended debate, language allowing any eventual House-Senate conference on the legislation to increase the debt limit. However, the Senate's supplemental appropriations bill (S. 2551; incorporated as an amendment to H.R. 4775, June 3, 2002) omitted debt-limit-increasing language. The Senate leadership expressed strong reluctance to include a debt limit increase in the supplemental appropriation bill. Instead, on June 11, the Senate adopted a bill (S. 2578), without debate, to raise the debt limit by $450 billion to $6,400 billion. At that time, a $450 billion debt limit increase was thought to provide enough borrowing authority for government operations through the rest of calendar year 2002, if not through the summer of 2003. With the possibility of default looming over it, the House passed the $450 billion debt limit increase by a single vote on June 27. The President signed the bill into law on June 28 (P.L. 107-199, 116 Stat. 734), ending the 2002 debt limit crisis.[37]

The Debt Limit Issue in 2003

On Christmas Eve, 2002, Kenneth Dam, Deputy Secretary of the Treasury sent a letter to Congress requesting an unspecified increase in the debt limit by late February 2003, signaling that the $6,400 billion debt limit would then be reached.[38] The 108th Congress, still in the process of organizing itself, did not immediately respond. Through the winter and into the spring, the Treasury repeatedly requested that the debt limit be raised to avoid serious financial problems. By February 20, 2003, the Treasury, as in 2002, used legislatively mandated measures to manage debt holdings of certain government accounts to avoid reaching the debt limit. These actions included the replacement of internally held government debt with non-debt instruments in certain government accounts and not issuing new debt to these accounts. These actions allowed the Treasury to issue additional debt to the public to acquire the cash needed to pay for the government's commitments or to issue new debt to other federal accounts.

Through the rest of February and into May, the Treasury held debt subject to limit $15 million below the debt ceiling.[39] The adoption of the conference report on the FY2004 budget resolution (H.Con.Res. 95; H.Rept. 108-71) on April 11, 2003, in the House triggered the "Gephardt rule" (House Rule XXVII) that deems to have passed legislation (in this case, H.J.Res. 51) raising the debt limit to accommodate the spending and revenue levels approved in the adopted budget resolution.[40]

The Senate received the debt-limit legislation on April 11, but did not act until May 23, after receiving further Treasury warnings of imminent default. On that day, debt subject to limit was $25 million (or 0.0004%) below the existing $6,400 billion limit. The Senate adopted the legislation, after rejecting eight amendments and sent it to the President, who signed it on May 27. This legislation raised the debt limit to $7,384 billion (P.L. 108-24, 117 Stat. 710).

The Debt Limit Issue in 2004

In January 2004, CBO estimated that the debt limit, then set at $7,384 billion, would be reached the following summer.[41] In June 2004, the Treasury asked Congress to raise the debt limit in order to avoid the disruptions to government finances experienced in the previous two years.[42] In August, and again in September, the Treasury declared that the debt limit would be reached in the first half of October. On October 14, debt subject to limit reached

$7,383,975 million, just $25 million below the existing limit. The Treasury employed methods used in the previous two years to keep debt under the legal limit. On October 14, Secretary of the Treasury John Snow informed Congress, just before the election recess, that available measures to avoid breaching the debt limit would be exhausted by mid-November.[43] Without an increase in the debt limit, the Treasury would be unable to meet all of the government's existing obligations, which could undermine the U.S. government's reputation in capital markets and raise costs of federal borrowing.

Although the House passed a budget resolution for FY2005 in the spring of 2004, it did not reach final agreement with the Senate on the measure. Without a budget resolution passed by Congress, no resolution to raise the debt limit could be deemed passed by the House automatically under the Gephardt rule. Consequently, no measure was available to send to the Senate. As the debt approached the limit through the summer and into the fall, no legislation was moved to raise the debt limit.

Earlier, in September 2004, the House had added an amendment to the FY2005 Transportation-Treasury appropriations (H.R. 5025) in an effort to remove the Treasury's flexibility in financing the government as federal debt approached and reached the existing limit. Without that flexibility, the government would be unable to meet its financial obligations as the amount of debt neared the limit. The legislation cleared the House, but the Senate did not act on it.

After the elections, Senator Frist, on November 16, 2004, introduced legislation (S. 2986) to raise the debt limit by $800 billion, from $7,384 billion to $8,184 billion. The Senate approved the increase on November 17, 2004. The House considered and approved the increase on November 18. The President signed the legislation into law (P.L. 108-415, 118 Stat. 2337) on November 19, 2004. Estimates made at that time anticipated the new limit would be reached between August and December 2005.

Shortly before the increase in the debt limit, the Treasury delayed a debt auction and informed Congress that it would invoke a "debt limit suspension period" as it had in previous years. The increase in the debt limit in mid-November allowed the Treasury to reschedule the debt auction and cancel, before it began, the "debt limit suspension period."

The Debt Limit Issue in 2005, 2006, and 2007

Debt limit increases in 2005, 2006, and 2007 took a less dramatic path than those in President Bush's first term. In 2005, Congress included three reconciliation instructions in the FY2006 budget resolution (H.Con.Res. 95, 109th Congress; April 28, 2005), the third of which directed the House Committee on Ways and Means and the Senate Finance Committee to report bills raising the debt limit. The instructions specified a $781 billion debt limit increase, to $8,965 billion, with a reporting date of no later than September 30, 2005. Neither committee reported a bill to raise the debt limit.

The adoption of the conference report on the FY2006 budget resolution in late April 2005 also triggered the Gephardt rule (House Rule XXVII), producing a House Joint Resolution (H.J.Res. 47) that also would raise the debt limit by $781 billion to $8,965 billion. Under the rule, the resolution was automatically deemed passed by the House and sent to the Senate. Through the end of the first session of the 109th Congress, the Senate had not considered H.J.Res. 47, nor had Congress considered a reconciliation bill raising the debt limit as called for in the budget resolution.

At the end of December 2005, Secretary of the Treasury Snow wrote Congress that the debt limit would probably be reached in mid-February 2006, although the Treasury could take actions that maintain the debt below its limit until mid-March. He therefore requested an increase in the debt limit.[44] In two more letters, sent on February 19 and March 6, Secretary Snow advised Congress that the Treasury was taking measures within its legal discretion to avoid reaching the limit and that these measures would suffice only until the middle of March 2006. Secretary Snow authorized actions used previously by the Treasury, including declaring a debt issuance suspension period. As March began, the government was again close to becoming unable to meet its obligations. During the week of March 13 the Senate took up H.J.Res. 47. On March 16, the Senate passed a debt limit increase after rejecting several amendments. The President's signature on March 20, 2006, then raised the debt limit (P.L. 109-182) to $8,965 billion.

In mid-May 2007, Congress passed the conference report (H.Rept. 110-153) on the FY2008 budget resolution. The House's Gephardt rule, triggered by the adoption of the conference report on the budget resolution, resulted in the automatic engrossment of a joint resolution (in this case, H.J.Res. 43, 110th Congress) raising the debt limit by $850 billion to $9,815 billion, and sending it to the Senate. At the end of July 2007, the Treasury asked Congress to raise the debt limit, stating the limit would be reached in early October 2007. In

August, the CBO Director said that projections suggested that the limit would be reached in late October or early November. Without an increase, the Treasury indicated that it would take steps within its legal authority to avoid exceeding the debt limit. The Senate Finance Committee approved the House resolution (H.J.Res. 43) without changes on September 12, 2007. The Senate then passed the measure on September 27, which the President signed on September 29, 2007 (P.L. 110-91).

The Economic Slowdown and Federal Debt

Fiscal Policy Considerations

The U.S. economy is currently recovering slowly from a severe economic recession that began in December 2007 and ended in June 2009.[45] The economic slowdown began with a rapid deceleration of housing prices and a rise in interest rate spreads between private lending rates and benchmark Federal Reserve rates, indicating an increasing reluctance of major financial institutions to lend to each other as well as to firms and individuals. This led to sharply higher federal deficit spending in FY2008 spurred by several major actions taken by Congress to unfreeze credit markets, boost consumption, and increase spending. Deficit spending was even higher in FY2009, with higher than average deficits as a percentage of GDP persisting into the next decade, likely leading to further increases in the federal debt and debt limit. While deficits for FY2010 were slightly lower and fiscal conditions are projected to improve in FY2011, deficits remain high relative to historical experience.

Economic recession affects the federal deficit in several ways. First, falling prices of many assets and equities can sharply reduce federal revenues from capital gains taxes and from the corporate tax. Second, individual income taxes, the largest component of federal revenues, may also fall if jobs are cut and unemployment increases due to economic conditions. Third, "automatic stabilizers" such as unemployment insurance and income support programs pay out more money as unemployment rises and the number of households eligible for means-tested benefits rises, thus increasing federal spending.

Boosting the economy through deficit spending provides a fiscal stimulus if the output levels of goods and services produced in the nation are below their potential levels. Deficit spending, however, can help accelerate inflation if output levels are near or at potential levels, and in addition, exacerbates long-term fiscal challenges. Several economists have expressed concerns that inflation, which had been relatively low since the early 1980s, could accelerate due to rising prices of food, energy, and primary commodities. While inflation would reduce the market value of the federal deficit, it would require Treasury to pay higher nominal interest rates on federal debt. The U.S. economy, however, is currently operating well below its potential, which has kept inflation at lower levels.

Raising the Debt Ceiling in 2008, 2009, and 2010

In a March 2008 report, CBO estimated the President's budget would lead to a $396 billion deficit in FY2008 and a $342 billion deficit in FY2009.[46] The actual deficit for FY2008 reached $455 billion. In August 2009, CBO estimated the deficit would total $1,587 billion in FY2009 and $1,381 billion in FY2010.[47] As a result of the current economic conditions and the actions of the federal government to bring the economy out of recession, the federal debt limit was raised twice in the second half of 2008 and twice in 2009.

The House Concurrent Resolution on the Budget (H.Con.Res. 312) recommended policies that would result in a $10,200 billion debt in FY2009. The Senate Concurrent Resolution on the Budget S.Con.Res. 70) recommended policies that would result in a total debt of $10,278 billion in FY2009.[48] Implementing either set of policies would require an increase in the federal debt limit. The conference agreement (H.Rept. 110-659) also recommended spending levels that would lead to a debt subject to limit of $10,207 billion in FY2009, a level that would require an increase in the statutory debt limit. The budget conference report passed the Senate on a 48-45 vote on June 4, 2008. The House passed the measure on the next day by a 214-210 vote. Agreement on the FY2009 budget resolution automatically created and deemed passed in the House legislation (H.J.Res. 92) that would increase the debt limit from its current level of $9,815 billion to $10,615 billion. Because the Senate did not take up H.J.Res. 92, the debt limit remained at $9,815 billion.

Subsequently, the House passed an amended version of the Housing and Economic Recovery Act of 2008 (H.R. 3221) by a vote of 272-152 that included a debt limit increase to $10,615 billion on July 23, 2008. The Senate then passed the measure on July 26 on a 72-13 vote. The President signed the bill on July 30 (P.L. 110-289), increasing the debt limit. In addition to increasing the debt limit, the act also contained provisions that would temporarily authorize the Secretary of Treasury to extend a line of credit to mortgage guarantee agencies Freddie Mac and Fannie Mae. The act also created the a new independent agency called the Federal Housing Finance Agency (FHFA), which replaced the Department of Housing and Urban

Development Office of Federal Housing Enterprise Oversight (OFHEO) and the Federal Housing Finance Board (FHFB).

While CBO indicated that it was more likely than not that such intervention would not be needed, it also estimated a 5% chance of a cost to taxpayers of more than $100 billion.[49] Because debt subject to limit was just $339 billion less than the debt ceiling of $9,815 billion when the Senate passed H.R. 3221, some financial market participants may have worried that the debt limit, without an increase, might have hindered the Treasury Secretary's ability to intervene to support Freddie Mac and Fannie Mae. On September 7, 2008, the FHFA placed Fannie Mae and Freddie Mac in conservatorship, providing FHFA with the full powers to control the assets and operations of the firms.

Since the deprivatization of Fannie Mae and Freddie Mac, the federal government has acted to provide stability to financial markets.[50] On September 20, 2008, the U.S. Treasury submitted a proposal to Congress to authorize the Treasury Secretary to buy mortgage-related assets in order to stabilize financial markets. The Treasury proposal would allow Treasury holdings of mortgage-related securities up to $700 billion and would raise the debt limit to $11,315 billion.[51] The House introduced the Emergency Economic Stabilization Act of 2008 (H.R. 3997), which incorporated the main tenets of the Treasury proposal including raising the debt limit to $11,315 billion.[52] On September 29, 2008, however, the House rejected this measure. On October 1, 2008, the Senate voted on, and passed, a different version of the Emergency Economic Stabilization Act of 2008 (H.R. 1424) that included the same debt limit increase.[53] The House passed H.R. 1424 on October 3, 2008, and it was signed into law by the President (P.L. 110-343) on the same day, raising the debt limit to $11,315 billion.

Current economic conditions led Congress to consider another economic stimulus measure. This measure contains both tax cuts and spending increases, which will increase the deficit by reducing revenues and increasing outlays. The American Recovery and Reinvestment Act of 2009 (ARRA) as passed by the Senate on February 10, 2009 (Division B of the Senate Substitute amendment to H.R. 1 and S. 350), contained a provision which would raise the debt limit to $12,140 billion. The version of this legislation originally passed by the House omitted this provision. The final conference agreement on ARRA was passed by the House and Senate on February 13, 2009, and signed by the President on February 17, 2009 (P.L. 111-5). This measure contained a provision increasing the debt limit to $12,104 billion.

The conference report on the Concurrent Resolution on the Budget for FY2010 (S.Con.Res. 13) recommended policies that would lead to a debt subject to limit of $13,233 billion in FY2010, a level that would require an increase in the statutory debt limit. The budget resolution also contained a revised estimate of debt subject to limit of $12,016 billion for FY2009. The adoption of this conference report on April 29, 2009, triggered the Gephardt rule (House Rule XXVII), producing a House Joint Resolution (H.J.Res. 45) that would raise the debt limit by $925 billion to $13,029 billion. Under the rule, the resolution was automatically deemed passed by the House and sent to the Senate.

In August 2009, according to media reports, Secretary of Treasury Timothy Geithner notified Congress that the debt limit would be reached in mid-October.[54] On November 4, the U.S. Treasury announced that it could postpone the time when federal debt would reach its statutory limit until the middle or the end of December. [55] Treasury dropped nearly $185 billion from its balance sheet by reducing the amount of loans available through the Supplemental Financing Program, an emergency loan program created in the days following Lehman Brothers' bankruptcy, from $200 billion to $15 billion, which extended the time until the debt limit would be reached.[56] According to media reports, the Obama Administration also contemplated scaling back the Troubled Asset Relief Program (TARP), which could also lower federal debt subject to statutory limit. Repayments of TARP funds by major financial institutions could also lower the amount of debt subject to limit.[57] Other measures, such as those taken in 2003 during a "debt issuance suspension period" (described above), could also have extended the U.S. Treasury's ability to operate within the debt limit. On the other hand, the U.S. Treasury was scheduled to issue $48 billion of nonmarketable securities to the FDIC on December 30 and to make interest payments to various federal trust funds on December 31 totaling about $100 billion, according to Wall Street analysts, which in the absence of a debt limit increase, could have challenged Treasury's debt management activities in the absence of special accounting measures.[58]

In mid-December, according to media reports, senior Members of the House chose to forgo a larger increase in the debt limit in favor of a smaller increase in the debt limit that would allow the U.S. Treasury Department to continue normal debt management operations for two months or so.[59] H.R. 4314, a measure to raise the debt limit to $12,394 billion, was introduced on December 15, 2009, and passed by the House the next day on a 218-214 vote.

Table 2 summarizes the increases in the debt limit since 1993.[66]

Table 2. Increases in the Debt Limit Since 1993

Date	Public Law (P.L.) Number	New Debt Limit ($ billion)	Change From Previous Limit ($ billion)
April 6, 1993	P.L. 103-12	$4,370a	$225
August 10, 1993	P.L. 103-33	4,900	530
February 8, 1996	P.L. 104-103	(b)	—
March 12, 1996	P.L. 104-115	(c)	—
March 29, 1996	P.L. 104-121	5,500	600d
August 5, 1997	P.L. 105-33	5,950	450
June 28, 2002	P.L. 107-199	6,400	450
May 27, 2003	P.L. 108-24	7,384	984
Nov. 19, 2004	P.L. 108-415	8,184	800
Date	Public Law (P.L.) Number	New Debt Limit ($ billion)	Change From Previous Limit ($ billion)
Mar. 20, 2006	P.L. 109-182	8,965	781
Sept. 29, 2007	P.L. 110-91	9,815	850
July 30, 2008	P.L. 110-289	10,615	800
Oct. 3, 2008	P.L. 110-343	11,315	700
Feb. 17, 2009	P.L. 111-5	12,104	789
Dec. 28, 2009	P.L. 111-123	12,394	290
February 12, 2010	P.L. 111-139	14,294	1,900

Source: CRS, compiled using the Legislative Information System, available at httpi/www.congress; OMB.

a Increased the debt limit temporarily through September 30, 1993.

b Temporarily exempted from limit obligations in an amount equal to the monthly insurance benefits payable under Title II of the Social Security Act in March 1996, the exemption to expire on the earlier of an increase in the limit or March 15, 1996.

c Temporarily exempted from limit (a) obligations in an amount equal to the monthly insurance benefits payable under Title II of the Social Security Act in March 1996 and (b) certain obligations issued to trust funds and other Federal Government accounts, both exemptions to expire on the earlier of an increase in the limit or March 30, 1996.

d Difference from debt limit set on August 10, 1983.

The Senate passed it on December 24 by a 60-39 vote, and the President signed the measure on December 28. On January 28, the Senate passed an amended version of H.J.Res. 45 on a 60-39 vote. The measure would raise the debt ceiling by $1,900 billion, to $14,294 billion.[60] In addition, one amendment to impose certain pay-as-you-go (PAYGO) restrictions was approved on a 60-40 vote.[61]

Some Members of Congress have called for the creation of a national commission to address federal debt and the government's fiscal situation, which could be enabled through a measure linked to an increase in the debt limit.[62] An amendment (S.Amdt. 3302 to S.Amdt. 3299) to H.J.Res. 45 that would have established a "Bipartisan Task Force for Responsible Fiscal Action" was not approved on a 53-46 vote, having failed to reach 60 votes, on January 26, 2010. President Obama then charged a National Commission on Fiscal Responsibility and Reform (Fiscal Commission) with identifying "policies to improve the fiscal situation in the medium term and to achieve fiscal sustainability over the long run."[63] The Fiscal Commission issued a report on December 1, 2010, and several commissioners issued their own fiscal proposals as well.[64]

The House approved H.J.Res. 45 on a 233-187 vote on February 4, forwarding the measure to the President. The Obama Administration had previously voiced its strong support for a debt limit increase.[65] The President signed the measure (P.L. 111-139) on February 12, 2010.

Deficit Estimates

The size of the debt may remain a concern in the future due to the size of impending federal deficits necessitating further increases in the debt limit. CBO warns that the current trajectory of federal borrowing is unsustainable and could lead to slower economic growth in the long run as debt rises as a percentage of GDP. The total federal deficit rose from $455 billion in FY2008 to $1,413 billion in FY2009, and is estimated to reach $1,342 billion in FY2010.[67] Much of the increase in deficits can be attributed to weak economic and financial market turmoil that started in late 2007, as well as to federal responses. Nonetheless, many budget experts remain concerned that a slow economic recovery or a "double-dip" recession could keep federal revenues below previous trendline projections for several years, and that the federal government would continue to run large deficits.

CONCLUDING COMMENTS

Since the late 1950s, the federal government increased its borrowing from the public in all years, except in FY1969 following imposition of a war surcharge and in the period FY1997-FY2001. The persistence of federal budget deficits has required the government to issue more and more debt to the public.[68] The accumulation of Social Security and other trust funds, particularly after 1983 when recommendations of the Greenspan Commission were implemented, led to sustained growth in government-held debt subject to limit.[69] The growth in federal debt held by the public and in intergovernmental accounts, such as trust funds, has periodically obliged Congress to raise the debt limit.

Between August 1997, when the debt limit was raised to $5,950 billion, and the beginning of FY2002 in October 2001, federal budget surpluses reduced debt held by the public. From the end of FY2001, the last fiscal year with a surplus, until the end of FY2008, debt held by the public subject to limit grew by $2,484 billion. Federal debt held in intergovernmental accounts grew steadily throughout the period, rising by $1,743 billion since the beginning of FY2002.

In early 2001, the 10-year budget forecasts projected large and growing surpluses, indicating rapid reduction in debt held by the public. Some experts expressed concern about consequences of retiring all federal debt held by the public.[70] Most long-term forecasts computed at that time, however, showed large deficits emerging once the baby boomers began to retire. Short-term forecasts projected continuous growth in debt held by government accounts, largely due to the difference between Social Security tax revenues and benefit payments. The combination of falling levels of publicly held debt and rising levels of debt held by government accounts moderated the expected growth of total debt. The moderate growth in total debt those projections had forecast was expected to postpone the need to increase the debt limit until late into the decade, when accumulating debt in government accounts would overtake reductions in debt held by the public.

New budget projections released in early 2002 smashed expectations of large, persistent surpluses, and hopes for reductions in debt held by the public collapsed. The return to large federal deficits accelerated the growth of total debt. Increases in the debt limit would be necessary much sooner than previously expected.

Early in 2003, the FY2003 deficit and the persistent rise in debt held by government accounts drove the federal debt up to the $6,400 billion limit in effect at the time. The Treasury avoided breaching the limit into May. Congress adopted a debt limit increase of $934 billion on May 23, 2003, that provided enough room for the growing federal debt through the fall of 2004. The debt limit increase passed by Congress late in 2004 was expected, at the time, to accommodate the government's debt growth well into 2005, if not into early 2006. In late December 2005, and early in 2006, the Treasury informed Congress that the limit would be reached between mid-February and mid-March 2006. On March 16, 2006, the Senate passed the House-initiated debt limit increase, raising the debt limit to $8,965 billion. The debt limit crisis was resolved when the President signed the debt limit increase on March 20.

Smaller than expected deficits in FY2006 and FY2007 postponed, but did not end the need for a new, higher debt limit. The House passed legislation in May 2007 (H.J.Res. 43) to raise the debt limit. The Senate passed the measure (P.L. 110-91) on September 27, which the President signed on September 29. Turmoil in some financial markets in August 2007, according to some observers, appeared to constrain contention over the debt limit increase.

The 2008 economic slowdown, which reduced federal tax revenues and increased federal outlays, caused federal deficit spending to rise, thus bringing forward the projected date when the federal debt will reach its current limit. The House passed an amended version of the Housing and Economic Recovery Act of 2008 (H.R. 3221) that included a debt limit increase to $10,615 billion on July 23, 2008. The Senate passed the measure on July 26, and the President signed it on July 30, raising the debt limit for the first time in 2008. Subsequently, the Emergency Economic Stabilization Act of 2008 (H.R. 1424), signed into law on October 3 (P.L. 110-343), raised the debt limit for the second time in 2008 to $11,315 billion. The debt limit was raised for the third time in less than a year as a result of passage of the American Recovery and Reinvestment Act of 2009. President Obama signed this measure on February 17, 2009 (P.L. 111-5), which raised the debt limit to $12,104 billion.

The debt limit was again raised in late 2009. H.R. 4314, passed by the House on December 16, 2009, and by the Senate on December 24, raised the debt limit to $12,394 billion when the President signed the measure on December 28. In early 2010, Congress voted for a larger increase in the debt limit, which would put the limit at $14,294 billion, raising the debt ceiling by $1,900 billion. President Obama signed the measure on February 12, 2010. This debt limit, according to projections, will allow the Treasury Department to issue new debt at projected levels until spring 2011.

Amendments offered during consideration of the latest debt limit increase may signal a growing concern with the fiscal sustainability. One amendment, which was not approved, would have established a statutory commission to consider long-term fiscal issues. Another amendment, which was approved, would impose certain PAYGO restrictions.[71] Over the next decade, without major changes in federal policies, persistent and possibly growing deficits, along with the ongoing growth in the debt holdings of government accounts, would increase substantially the amount of federal debt subject to limit. Unless federal policies change, Congress would repeatedly face demands to raise the debt limit to accommodate the growing federal debt in order to provide the government with the means to meet its financial obligations.

Further Reading

Drishnakumar, Anita S., "In Defense of the Debt Limit Statute," *Harvard Journal on Legislation*, vol. 42, 2005, pp. 135-185.

Gordon, John Steele, Hamilton's Blessing: the Extraordinary Life and Times of Our National Debt, New York: Penguin, 1998.

Hormats, Robert D., The Price of Liberty: Paying for America's Wars from the Revolution to the War on Terror, New York: Times Books, 2007.

Noll, Franklin, "The United States Public Debt, 1861 to 1975," EH.Net Encyclopedia, edited by Robert Whaples, May 26, 2004. Available at http://eh.net/encyclopedia/article/noll.publicdebt.

Wright, Robert E., One Nation Under Debt: Hamilton, Jefferson, and the History of What We Owe, New York: McGraw-Hill, 2008.

Appendix. Debt Subject to Limit by Month Since September 2001

Table A-1 provides data on the dollar amount, in current dollars, of federal debt and the changes in these amounts by month between the end of September 2001 (the end of FY2001) and the end of December 2010. The table shows outstanding monthly balances, subject to the debt limit, of total federal debt, debt held by government accounts, and debt held by the public.

All three measures of debt subject to limit increased over this period. From the end of September 2001 (the end of FY2001) to the end of September 2010 (the most recently completed fiscal year), total federal debt increased by $7,778 billion, debt held in government accounts increased by $2,073 billion, and debt held by the public increased by $5,705 billion. All three measures experienced periodic reductions in some months. Because federal receipts and outlays are spread unevenly over the fiscal year, debt may rise or fall in a given month, even if debt measures follow an overall increasing trend.

Table A-1. Debt Subject to Limit by Month, September 2001-December 2010 (in millions of current dollars)

End of Month	Total	Change from Previous Period	Held by Government Accounts	Change from Previous Period	Held by the Public	Change from Previous Period
Sept. 2001	$5,732,802	—	$2,436,521	—	$3,296,281	—
Oct. 2001	5,744,523	$11,721	2,451,815	$15,294	3,292,709	$-3,572
Nov. 2001	5,816,823	72,300	2,469,647	17,832	3,347,176	54,467
Dec. 2001	5,871,413	54,590	2,516,012	46,365	3,355,401	8,225
Jan. 2002	5,865,892	-5,521	2,525,755	9,743	3,340,138	-15,263
Feb. 2002	5,933,154	67,262	2,528,494	2,739	3,404,659	64,521
Mar. 2002	5,935,108	1,954	2,528,318	-176	3,406,789	2,130
Apr. 2002	5,914,816	-20,292	2,549,438	21,120	3,365,378	-41,411
May 2002	5,949,975	35,159	2,553,350	3,912	3,396,625	31,247
June 2002	6,058,313	108,338	2,630,646	77,296	3,427,667	31,042
July 2002	6,092,050	33,737	2,627,980	-2,666	3,464,070	36,403
Aug. 2002	6,142,835	50,785	2,620,946	-7,034	3,521,890	57,820
Sept. 2002	6,161,431	18,596	2,644,244	23,298	3,517,187	-4,703
Oct. 2002	6,231,284	69,853	2,680,812	36,568	3,550,472	33,285
Nov. 2002	6,294,480	63,196	2,680,788	-24	3,613,692	63,220
Dec. 2002	6,359,412	64,932	2,745,787	64,999	3,613,625	-67

Table A-1. (Continued)

End of Month	Total	Change from Previous Period	Held by Government Accounts	Change from Previous Period	Held by the Public	Change from Previous Period
Jan. 2003	6,355,812	-3,600	2,753,301	7,514	3,602,511	-11,114
Feb. 2003	6,399,975	44,163	2,750,471	-2,830	3,649,504	46,993
Mar. 2003	6,399,975	0	2,722,812	-27,659	3,677,163	27,659
Apr. 2003	6,399,975	0	2,731,042	8,230	3,668,933	-8,230
May 2003	6,498,658	98,683	2,755,895	24,853	3,742,763	73,830
June 2003	6,625,519	126,861	2,842,361	86,466	3,783,158	40,395
July 2003	6,704,814	79,295	2,835,566	-6,795	3,869,247	86,089
Aug. 2003	6,743,775	38,961	2,829,387	-6,179	3,914,388	45,141
Sept. 2003	6,737,553	-6,222	2,846,730	17,343	3,890,823	-23,565
Oct. 2003	6,826,668	89,115	2,869,493	22,763	3,957,175	66,352
Nov. 2003	6,879,626	52,958	2,879,117	9,624	4,000,509	43,334
Dec. 2003	6,952,893	73,267	2,940,736	61,619	4,012,157	11,648
Jan. 2004	6,966,851	13,958	2,951,219	10,483	4,015,633	3,476
Feb. 2004	7,049,163	82,312	2,953,123	1,904	4,096,040	80,407
Mar. 2004	7,088,648	39,485	2,941,195	-11,928	4,147,453	51,413
Apr. 2004	7,089,700	1,052	2,960,151	18,956	4,129,549	-17,904
May 2004	7,151,523	61,823	2,973,869	13,718	4,177,653	48,104
June 2004	7,229,320	77,797	3,039,987	66,118	4,189,334	11,681
July 2004	7,271,328	42,008	3,033,396	-6,591	4,237,933	48,599
Aug. 2004	7,305,531	34,203	3,037,149	3,753	4,268,382	30,449
Sept. 2004	7,333,350	27,819	3,056,590	19,441	4,276,760	8,378

End of Month	Total	Change from Previous Period	Held by Government Accounts	Change from Previous Period	Held by the Public	Change from Previous Period
Oct. 2004	7,383,975	50,625	3,096,207	39,617	4,287,768	11,008
Nov. 2004	7,464,740	80,765	3,087,834	-8,373	4,376,906	89,138
Dec. 2004	7,535,644	70,904	3,158,531	70,697	4,377,114	208
Jan. 2005	7,567,702	32,058	3,171,089	12,558	4,396,615	19,501
Feb. 2005	7,652,726	85,024	3,176,406	5,317	4,476,320	79,705
Mar. 2005	7,715,503	62,777	3,175,460	-946	4,540,042	63,722
Apr. 2005	7,704,041	-11,462	3,185,364	9,904	4,518,677	-21,365
May 2005	7,717,574	13,533	3,207,232	21,868	4,510,342	-8,335
June 2005	7,778,128	60,554	3,280,914	73,682	4,497,214	-13,128
July 2005	7,829,029	50,901	3,278,725	-2,189	4,550,304	53,090
Aug. 2005	7,868,395	39,366	3,284,696	5,971	4,583,699	33,395
Sept. 2005	7,871,040	2,645	3,300,969	16,273	4,570,071	-13,628
Oct. 2005	7,964,782	93,742	3,345,589	44,620	4,619,193	49,122
Nov. 2005	8,028,918	64,136	3,351,093	5,504	4,677,826	58,633
Dec. 2005	8,107,019	78,101	3,424,304	73,211	4,682,715	4,889
Jan. 2006	8,132,290	25,271	3,442,543	18,239	4,689,747	7,032
Feb. 2006	8,183,975	51,685	3,457,409	14,866	4,726,567	36,820
Mar. 2006	8,281,451	97,476	3,443,602	-13,807	4,837,849	111,282
Apr. 2006	8,262,718	-18,733	3,479,623	36,021	4,783,095	-54,754
May 2006	8,263,812	1,094	3,492,648	13,025	4,771,165	-11,930
June 2006	8,330,646	66,834	3,566,186	73,538	4,764,460	-6,705
July 2006	8,352,614	21,968	3,569,550	3,364	4,783,064	18,604

Table A-1. (Continued)

End of Month	Total	Change from Previous Period	Held by Government Accounts	Change from Previous Period	Held by the Public	Change from Previous Period
Aug. 2006	8,423,321	70,707	3,576,166	6,616	4,847,155	64,091
Sept. 2006	8,420,278	-3,043	3,622,378	46,212	4,828,972	-18,183
Oct. 2006	8,498,016	77,738	3,650,241	27,863	4,847,775	18,803
Nov. 2006	8,545,715	47,699	3,649,736	-505	4,895,979	48,204
Dec. 2006	8,592,513	46,798	3,724,450	74,714	4,868,063	-27,916
Jan. 2007	8,619,499	26,986	3,737,894	13,444	4,881,605	13,542
Feb. 2007	8,690,921	71,422	3,744,299	6,405	4,946,622	65,017
Mar. 2007	8,760,735	69,814	3,740,127	-4,172	5,020,608	73,986
Apr. 2007	8,753,070	-7,665	3,778,255	38,128	4,974,815	-45,793
May 2007	8,740,892	-12,178	3,792,201	13,946	4,948,691	-26,124
June 2007	8,779,168	38,276	3,867,819	75,618	4,911,348	-37,343
July 2007	8,845,417	66,249	3,873,239	5,420	4,972,178	60,830
Aug. 2007	8,918,493	73,076	3,854,115	-19,124	5,064,377	92,199
Sept. 2007	8,921,343	2,850	3,903,710	49,595	5,017,633	-46,744
Oct. 2007	8,994,639	73,296	3,958,357	54,647	5,036,281	18,648
Nov. 2007	9,065,827	71,188	3,950,468	-7,889	5,115,358	79,077
Dec. 2007	9,144,715	78,888	4,038,566	88,098	5,106,149	-9,209
Jan. 2008	9,155,842	11,127	4,053,199	14,633	5,102,644	-3,505
Feb. 2008	9,275,683	119,841	4,045,007	-8,192	5,230,676	128,032
Mar. 2008	9,358,135	82,452	4,051,685	6,678	5,306,450	75,774
Apr. 2008	9,298,567	-59,568	4,080,887	29,202	5,217,680	-88,770

End of Month	Total	Change from Previous Period	Held by Government Accounts	Change from Previous Period	Held by the Public	Change from Previous Period
May 2008	9,324,137	25,570	4,071,992	-8,895	5,252,144	34,464
June 2008	9,427,901	167,869	4,169,509	134,950	5,258,392	32,920
July 2008	9,520,220	92,319	4,144,377	-25,132	5,375,843	117,451
Aug. 2008	9,580,508	60,288	4,129,413	-14,964	5,451,095	75,252
Sept. 2008	9,959,850	379,342	4,179,574	50,161	5,780,276	329,181
Oct. 2008	10,504,702	544,852	4,231,878	52,304	6,272,824	492,548
Nov. 2008	10,595,725	91,023	4,228,270	-3,608	6,367,454	94,630
Dec. 2008	10,640,274	44,549	4,298,482	70,212	6,341,792	-25,662
Jan. 2009	10,569,310	-70,964	4,278,424	-20,058	6,290,886	-50,906
Feb. 2009	10,814,630	245,320	4,261,734	-16,690	6,552,896	262,010
Mar. 2009	11,066,217	251,587	4,258,272	-3,462	6,807,946	255,050
Apr. 2009	11,178,827	112,610	4,273,005	14,733	6,905,822	97,876
May 2009	11,260,445	81,618	4,265,719	-7,286	6,994,725	88,903
June 2009	11,487,470	227,025	4,336,673	70,954	7,150,797	156,072
July 2009	11,611,178	123,708	4,299,673	-37,000	7,311,505	160,708
Aug. 2009	11,755,205	144,027	4,294,923	-4,750	7,460,282	148,777
Sept. 2009	11,853,434	98,229	4,325,124	30,201	7,528,311	68,029
Oct. 2009	11,836,629	-16,805	4,372,308	47,184	7,464,321	-63,990
Nov. 2009	12,057,363	220,734	4,367,935	-4,373	7,689,428	225,107
Dec. 2009	12,254,506	197,143	4,466,279	98,344	7,788,227	98,799
Jan. 2010	12,222,507	-31,999	4,485,502	19,223	7,737,005	-51,222
Feb. 2010	12,383,717	161,210	4,469,373	-16,129	7,914,344	177,339

Table A-1. (Continued)

End of Month	Total	Change from Previous Period	Held by Government Accounts	Change from Previous Period	Held by the Public	Change from Previous Period
Mar. 2010	12,716,511	332,794	4,448,645	-20,728	8,267,866	353,522
Apr. 2010	12,892,729	176,218	4,480,458	31,813	8,412,271	144,405
May 2010	12,992,539	99,810	4,498,120	17,662	8,494,419	82,148
June 2010	13,149,560	157,021	4,537,716	39,596	8,611,844	117,425
July 2010	13,185,208	35,648	4,504,601	-33,115	8,680,607	68,763
Aug. 2010	13,398,794	213,586	4,493,418	-11,183	8,905,376	224,769
Sept. 2010	13,510,840	112,046	4,509,632	16,214	9,001,208	95,832
Oct. 2010	13,617,337	106,497	4,568,895	59,263	9,048,442	47,234
Nov. 2010	13,809,121	191,784	4,555,396	-13,499	9,253,725	205,283
Dec. 2010	13,972,513	163,392	4,603,888	48,492	9,368,625	114,900

Source: U.S. Treasury, Bureau of the Public Debt, *Monthly Statement of the Public Debt*, Sept. 2001-Nov. 2010, available at http://www.treasurydirect.gov/govt/reports/pd/mspd/mspd.htm; CRS calculations. Dec. 2010 data computed from Daily Treasury Statement.

End Notes

[1] Approximately 0.5% of total debt is excluded from debt limit coverage. The Treasury defines "Total Public Debt Subject to Limit" as "the Total Public Debt Outstanding less Unamortized Discount on Treasury Bills and Zero-Coupon Treasury Bonds, old debt issued prior to 1917, and old currency called United States Notes, as well as Debt held by the Federal Financing Bank and Guaranteed Debt." For details, see http://www.treasurydirect.gov. The debt limit is codified as 31 USC 3101.

[2] Although there are hundreds of trust funds, the overwhelming majority are very small. The 12 largest trust funds hold 98.8% of the federal debt held in government accounts.

[3] Other means of financing—including cash balance changes, seigniorage, and capitalization of financing accounts used to fund federal credit programs—have relatively little effect on the changes in debt held by the public.

[4] In future years, when some trust funds are projected to pay out more than they take in, funds that the Treasury would use to redeem those intergovernmental debts must be obtained via higher taxes or lower government spending.

[5] Trust fund surpluses by law must be invested in special federal government securities.

[6] Daily data on federal debt can be obtained at the Treasury Department's Bureau of the Public Debt website: http://www.treasurydirect.gov/NP/BPDLogin?application=np. Data on debt subject to limit are provided in the *Daily Treasury Statement*, available at http://fms.treas.gov/dts/index.html.

[7] U.S. Congressional Budget Office, *The Budget and Economic Outlook: An Update*, August 19, 2010, p. 1, available at http://www.cbo.gov/doc.cfm?index=11705.

[8] Wrightson ICAP, *The Money Market Observer*, December 13, 2010.

[9] Paul M. Krawzak, "Showdown Ahead on Debt Limit as Geithner Urges Action," *CQ Today Online News*, January 6, 2011; Secretary of the U.S. Treasury Timothy Geithner, letter to Majority Leader Harry Reid, dated January 6, 2011.

[10] For details, see the CRS congressional distribution memorandum *Reaching the Debt Limit*, December 28, 2010, coordinated by Mindy R. Levit. This memorandum is available upon request by congressional offices.

[11] 31 U.S.C. §3902.

[12] 26 U.S.C. §6611.

[13] For details, see archived CRS Report 95-1109, *Authority to Tap Trust Funds and Establish Payment Priorities if the Debt Limit is not Increased*, by Thomas J. Nicola and Morton Rosenberg. Available upon request from authors. 5 U.S.C. Sec. 8348(b) defines a debt issuance suspension period as "any period for which the Secretary of the Treasury determines for purposes of this subsection that the issuance of obligations of the United States may not be made without exceeding the public debt limit." After a debt issuance suspension period ends, the Treasury Secretary must report to Congress as soon as possible regarding fund balances and any extraordinary actions taken. For details, see 5 USC Sec. 8348(j,k).

[14] U.S. General Accounting Office (GAO), *Analysis of Actions Taken during the 2003 Debt Issuance Suspension Period,* GAO-04-526, May 2004, available at http://www.gao.gov/new.items/d04526.pdf.

[15] For a vigorous assertion of the utility of the debt ceiling, see Anita S. Drishnakumar, "In Defense of the Debt Limit Statute," *Harvard Journal on Legislation*, vol. 42, 2005, pp. 135-185.

[16] Marshall A. Robinson, *The National Debt Ceiling: An Experiment in Fiscal Policy*, Washington, DC: The Brookings Institution, 1959, p. 5.

[17] Bruce Bartlett, "Why Congress Must Now Abolish its Debt Limit," *Financial Times*, October 22, 2009, p. 11.

[18] P.L. 65-43, 40 Stat. 288, enacted September 24, 1917. Currently codified as amended as 31 U.S.C. § 3101.

[19] H. J. Cooke and M. Katzen, "The Public Debt Limit," *Journal of Finance*, vol. 9, no. 3 (September 1954), pp. 298-303.

[20] Robert D. Hormats, *The Price of Liberty,* (New York: Henry Holt, 2007), ch. 4.

[21] Treasury certificates of indebtedness were short-term, interest-bearing securities. Treasury bills are securities with a maturity of a year or less. Treasury notes are interest-bearing securities that generally have maturities of two to five years. Treasury bonds are interest-bearing securities that generally have maturities of 10 or more years.

[22] Marshall A. Robinson, *The National Debt Ceiling: An Experiment in Fiscal Policy*, (Washington, DC: The Brookings Institution, 1959), pp.1-6.

[23] The War Revenue Act, formally "An Act to Provide Ways and Means to Meet War Expenditures and for Other Purposes," was enacted June 13, 1898. Much of the legislative text of the Act's public borrowing sections (§32, 33) were drawn from the Acts of June 30, 1864, ch. 172, §1 (13 Stats. 218) and of March 3, 1865, ch. 77 (13 Stats. 469).

[24] Some opponents raised concerns that granting the Treasury Secretary authority to issue debt could affect monetary policies, which might tighten credit conditions. Such concerns became less relevant after the establishment of the Federal Reserve System in 1913. See House debate, *Congressional Record*, vol. 31, part 6 (June 9, 1898), pp. 5713-5728; and Senate debate on June 10, 1898, pp. 5734-5749.

[25] P.L. 76-201. Some authors claimed the aggregate limit was first created in Public Debt Act of 1941 (P.L. 77-7). The 1939 Senate floor debate, however, makes clear that Congress intended to lift categorical debt restrictions. See Senate debate, *Congressional Record*, vol. 84, part 6 (June 1, 1939), pp. 6480, 6497-6501.

[26] This limit did not apply to certain previous public debt issues that constituted a minor portion of the federal debt.

[27] U.S. Bureau of the Census, *Historical Statistics of the United States: Colonial Times to 1970*, H. Doc. 93-78 (Washington: GPO, 1975), Series Y 493-504.

[28] Public Debt Acts of 1941 (P.L. 77-7), 1942 (P.L. 77-510), 1943 (78-34), 1944 (P.L. 78-333), and 1945 (P.L. 79-48).

[29] U.S. Office of Management and Budget, FY2010 Budget of the U.S. Government: Historical Tables, Table 7-3.

[30] Until 2001, Treasury publications did not divide debt subject to limit by that held by the public and that held by government accounts. Table 1 uses CRS calculations that approximate levels of debt subject to limit held in these two categories for fiscal years prior to 2001.

[31] The data show components of debt compared to the size of the economy. This avoids possible distortions resulting from changing price levels over time and includes changes in per capita incomes. This percentage increases when debt grows faster than GDP and falls when it grows more slowly than GDP.

[32] Federal on-budget receipts and outlays nearly matched in FY1999, and the on-budget surplus in FY2000 was 0.9% of GDP. Prior to FY1999, the federal government last had an on-budget surplus in FY1960. Social Security receipts in excess of benefits make up most of the off-budget surplus, which has been positive since FY1985.

[33] U.S. Congress, Congressional Budget Office, An Analysis of the President's Budgetary Proposals for Fiscal Year 2009, March 2008, available at http://www.cbo.gov/ftpdocs/89xx/doc8990/03-19-AnalPresBudget.pdf.

[34] The debt limit was raised from $5,500 billion to $5,950 billion on August 5, 1997, as part of the Balanced Budget Act of 1997 (P.L. 105-33, 111 Stat. 251).

[35] For a comprehensive discussion of the Treasury's previous uses of its short-term ability to avoid breaching the debt limit, see U.S. General Accounting Office, *Debt Ceiling: Analysis of Actions During the 1995-1996 Crisis*, GAO/AIMD-96-130, August 1996.

[36] U.S. Department of the Treasury, Treasury News, *Treasury Statement on the Debt Ceiling*, May 14, 2002.

[37] For additional details, see U.S. General Accounting Office, *Debt Ceiling: Analysis of Actions During the 2002 Debt Issuance Suspension Period*, GAO-03-134, December 2002.

[38] Kenneth Dam, Deputy Secretary of the Treasury, letter to Speaker of the House, Dennis Hastert, December 24, 2002, available at http://www.treas.gov/press/releases/po3718.htm.

[39] The Treasury reduced the amount of debt held by selected federal accounts while it sold an equal (or smaller) amount of debt to the public. This raised cash needed to pay for ongoing obligations and kept the debt below the limit.

[40] The House Budget Committee has some discretion in setting the debt limit level in the House Joint resolution generated by the Gephardt rule. See CRS Report 98-453, *Debt-Limit Legislation in the Congressional Budget Process*, by Bill Heniff Jr. and CRS Report RL31913, *Developing Debt-Limit Legislation: The House's "Gephardt Rule"*, by Bill Heniff Jr..

[41] U.S. Congress, Congressional Budget Office, *The Budget and Economic Outlook: Fiscal Years 2005 to 2014*, January 2004.

[42] Alan Fram, "Congress May Duck Debt Limit Raise," *Oakland Tribune*, June 5, 2004.

[43] John W. Snow, Secretary of the U.S. Treasury, letter to Senate Majority Leader Bill Frist, October 14, 2004, available at http://www.treas.gov/press/releases/reports/frist.pdf.

[44] John W. Snow, Secretary of the Treasury, letter to Senator Max Baucus, December 29, 2005, available at http://www.ombwatch.org/files/budget/pdf/snow_debtlimit_2006.pdf.

[45] The end of a recession is said to occur when an economy has stopped shrinking, not when it has recovered. See National Bureau of Economic Research Business Cycle Dating Committee, press release, September 20, 2010, available at http://www.nber.org/cycles

[46] U.S. Congress, Congressional Budget Office, *An Analysis of the President's Budgetary Proposals for Fiscal Year 2009*, Table 1.1, March 2008, available at http://www.cbo.gov/ftpdocs/89xx/doc8990/03-19-AnalPresBudget.pdf.

[46] U.S. Congress, Congressional Budget Office, *The Budget and Economic Outlook: An Update*, Table 1-1, August 2009, available at http://www.cbo.gov/doc.cfm?index=10521.

[47] Goldman Sachs U.S. Research, "US Daily: The Fiscal 2008 Deficit—Likely to Top $500 Billion," March 25, 2008.

[48] U.S. Congress, House Committee on the Budget, *Report to Accompany H. Con. Res. 312*, 110th Cong., 2nd sess., H.Rept. 110-543, March 2008, p. 99; U.S. Congress, Senate Committee on the Budget, *Report to Accompany S. Res. 70*, S.Prt. 110-039, March 2008.

[49] U.S. Congress, Congressional Budget Office, Cost Estimate for H.R. 3221 "Housing and Economic Recovery Act of 2008" As passed by the Senate on July 11, 2008, with an amendment transmitted to CBO on July 22, 2008, July 24, 2008, available at http://www.cbo.gov/ftpdocs/95xx/doc9597/hr3221.pdf.

[50] For additional information see CRS Report RS22956, *The Cost of Government Financial Interventions, Past and Present*, by Baird Webel, Marc Labonte, and N. Eric Weiss.

[51] U.S. Department of Treasury, "Fact Sheet: Proposed Treasury Authority to Purchase Troubled Assets," Press release hp-1150, Sept. 20, 2008, available at http://www.treas.gov/press/releases/hp1150.htm.

[52] U.S. Congress, House Financial Services Committee, Emergency Economic Stabilization Act of 2008 (Amendment to the Senate Amendment to H.R. 3997), available at http://www.house.gov/apps/list/press/financialsvcs_dem/ amend_001_xml.pdf.

[53] U.S. Congress, Senate Banking, Housing, and Urban Affairs Committee, Emergency Economic Stabilization Act of 2008 (In the Nature of a Substitute to H.R. 1424), available at http://banking latestversionAYO08C32_xml.pdf.

[54] *CQ Weekly*, "Fall 2009 Outlook: Debt Limit Increase," September 7, 2009, p. 1966.

[55] U.S. Treasury, "November 2009 Quarterly Refunding Statement," press release tg346, November 4, 2009, http://www.ustreas.gov/press/releases/tg346.htm; David Clarke and CQ Staff, "Treasury Gives Congress More Breathing Room on Debt Limit," *CQ Today Online News*, November 4, 2009.

[56] For details, see Joseph Haubrich and John Lindner, "The Supplemental Financing Program," *Economic Trends,* Federal Reserve of Chicago, September 28, 2009, available at http://www.clevelandfed.org/research/trends/2009/1009/ 03monpol.cfm.
[57] The Money Market Observer: Wrightson ICAP's Weekly Newsletter, December 7, 2009.
[58] The Money Market Observer: Wrightson ICAP's Weekly Newsletter, November 30, 2009.
[59] Paul Kane, "House Democrats Discard Larger Debt Limit," *Washington Post*, December 15, 2009, p. A4.
[60] *CQ Today Midday Update*, "Senate Sends Debt Ceiling Increase to House," January 28, 2010.
[61] S.Amdt. 3305. A second amendment (S.Amdt. 3300), approved on a 97-0 vote, provides certain protections to the Social Security program. Other amendments were not approved.
[62] Jonathan Weisman and John D. McKinnon, "White House Weighs New Panel to Tackle Deficit: Bipartisan Commission Considered As Administration Seeks to Show Resolve on a Problem that Dogs Its Broader Agenda," *Wall Street Journal*, November 26, 2009, p. A10.
[63] Executive Order 13531, "National Commission on Fiscal Responsibility and Reform," February 18, 2010; 75 FR 7927, February 23, 2010.
[64] National Commission on Fiscal Responsibility and Reform, *The Moment of Truth*, report, December 1, 2010, available at http://www.fiscalcommission.gov/sites/ fiscalcommission.gov/files/documents/ TheMomentofTruth12_1_2010.pdf.
[65] U.S. Office of Management and Budget, "H.J.Res. 45—Increasing the Statutory Limit on the Public Debt," Statement Of Administration Policy, January 20, 2010, available at http://www.whitehouse.gov/omb/assets saphjr45s_20100120.pdf.
[66] For a discussion of earlier debt limit increases, see CRS Report 98-805 E, *Public Debt Limit Legislation: A Brief History and Controversies In the 1980s and 1990s*, by Philip D. Winters, which is available from the authors upon request.
[67] U.S. Congressional Budget Office, *The Budget and Economic Outlook: An Update*, August 19, 2010, p. 1, available at http://www.cbo.gov/doc.cfm?index=11705.
[68] The ability to run fiscal deficits gives the federal government useful flexibility in managing its finances, although large deficits may harm economic performance. See CRS Report RL33657, *Running Deficits: Positives and Pitfalls*, by D. Andrew Austin.
[69] *Report of the National Commission on Social Security Reform*, January 1983, available at http://www.ssa.gov/history/reports/gspan.html.
[70] Testimony of Federal Reserve Chairman Alan Greenspan, in U.S. Congress, Senate Committee on the Budget, *Outlook for the Federal Budget and Implications for Fiscal Policy*, hearings, 107th Cong., 1st sess., January 25, 2001, available at http://www.federalreserve.gov/ boarddocs/testimony/2001/20010125/default.htm.
[71] For a discussion of PAYGO in the past, see CRS Report R41005, *The Statutory PAYGO Process for Budget Enforcement: 1991-2002*, by Robert Keith.

INDEX

D

E

F

G

H

I

R

S